WHO WERE THE BABYLONIANS?

SBL

Society of Biblical Literature

Archaeology and Biblical Studies

Andrew G. Vaughn,
Editor

Number 10

WHO WERE THE BABYLONIANS?

WHO WERE THE BABYLONIANS?

by
Bill T. Arnold

Society of Biblical Literature
Atlanta

WHO WERE THE BABYLONIANS?

Copyright © 2004 by the Society of Biblical Literature

Library of Congress Cataloging-in-Publication Data

Arnold, Bill T.
    Who were the Babylonians? / by Bill T. Arnold.
        p. cm. — (Archaeology and biblical studies / Society of Biblical Literature ; no. 10)
        Includes bibliographical references and indexes.
    ISBN 1-58983-106-3 (paper binding : alk. paper)
    1. Babylonia—History. I. Title. II. Series: Archaeology and biblical studies ; no. 10.
    DS73.2 .A73 2004b
    935.02—dc22   2004022881

12 11 10 09 08 07 06 05 04   5 4 3 2 1

Printed in the United States of America on acid-free, recycled paper conforming to ANSI/NISO Z39.48-1992 (R1997) and ISO 9706:1994 standards for paper permanence.

CONTENTS

PREFACE

When ancient classical historians such as Herodotus and Berossus mention the Babylonians, or when authors of the Bible speak of the Babylonians, to what or whom do they refer? My task in this volume is to trace briefly the geopolitical realities behind these literary references in light of the most recent Assyriological data and, more broadly, to present a compendium of our knowledge of the ancient Babylonians—in short, to answer the question, Who were the Babylonians?

The history of Babylonia has often been written by archaeologists *for* archaeologists or by philologists *for* philologists. Specialists, writing mostly for each other, have investigated all areas of Mesopotamia's material culture or impressive cuneiform documentary evidence. While these approaches have their distinct contributions (indeed, I am indebted to them, as the notes will show), my objective is to provide a more general survey for students of history, archaeology, philology, and the Bible. Consequently, my approach will be broader and at the same time more specifically focused on Babylonia and the Babylonians rather than on ancient Mesopotamia per se.

Chronological precision is still impossible for most of Babylonian history prior to the first millennium B.C.E. For the earliest periods, and especially for the troublesome Old Babylonian chronology, I have continued to follow the so-called "Middle Chronology," which has given us the familiar dates for Hammurapi, 1792–1750 B.C.E.[1] However, despite its wide acceptance in the secondary literature, the Middle Chronology is far from certain and has come under recent scrutiny.[2] The reader should be aware that the chronological schema used here for the third and second millennia B.C.E. are extremely tentative. Greater precision is possible for the first millennium B.C.E., although the complexities of the use of a lunar calendar in Mesopotamia and the Levant resulted in intercalary months, which was handled differently in each culture.[3] Thus, we are seldom in a position to speak with certainty on chronological issues, even for the later periods.

I am grateful to Andrew Gilmore, my research assistant, for his invaluable help with a number of points, as well as to Andrew Vaughn and Bob Buller for their patient guidance. I am also grateful to Sujatha Pichamuthu for her help with the maps.

As I finished the manuscript for this book, the politics of the Middle East were ever-present in the daily news. Since the 1980s, much archaeological excavation shifted focus from southern Mesopotamia to Syria in the northwest, largely because of the political situation in Iraq. Now, as Iraq itself struggles to emerge from postwar devastation, it can only be hoped that opportunities for further research of Iraq's heritage will become a reality and will contribute to the reconstruction of that great land. It is the earnest hope of all students of Iraq's cultural past that the people of Iraq will enjoy a future as bright and peaceful as that past was glorious.

ABBREVIATIONS

AB	Anchor Bible
ABD	*Anchor Bible Dictionary*. Edited by David Noel Freedman. 6 vols. New York: Doubleday, 1992.
ABRL	Anchor Bible Reference Library
ADAJ	*Annual of the Department of Antiquities of Jordan*
AfO	*Archiv für Orientforschung*
Ag. Ap.	Josephus, *Against Apion*
AHw	*Akkadisches Handwörterbuch*. Wolfram von Soden. 3 vols. Wiesbaden: Harrassowitz, 1965–81.
AJA	*American Journal of Archaeology*
ANET	*Ancient Near Eastern Texts Relating to the Old Testament*. Edited by James B. Pritchard. 3d ed. Princeton, N.J.: Princeton University Press, 1969.
Ant.	Josephus, *Antiquities*
AnOr	Analecta orientalia
AOAT	Alter Orient und Altes Testament
AOS	American Oriental Series
AS	Assyriological Studies
BaghM	*Baghdader Mitteilungen*
BASOR	*Bulletin of the American Schools of Oriental Research*
BMes	Bibliotheca mesopotamica
BO	*Bibliotheca orientalis*
BZAW	Beihefte zur Zeitschrift für die alttestamentliche Wissenschaft
CAD	*The Assyrian Dictionary of the Oriental Institute of the University of Chicago*. Edited by A. Leo Oppenheim et al. Chicago: University of Chicago Press, 1956–.
CAH	*The Cambridge Ancient History*. Edited by I. E. S. Edwards and John Boardman. 14 vols. Cambridge: Cambridge University Press, 1970–.
CANE	*Civilizations of the Ancient Near East*. Edited by J. Sasson. 4 vols. New York: Scribner, 1995.
CBQ	*Catholic Biblical Quarterly*

COS   *The Context of Scripture.* Edited by William W. Hallo and
               K. L. Younger. 3 vols. Leiden: Brill, 1997–2002.
DDD   *Dictionary of Deities and Demons in the Bible.* Edited by
               Karel van der Toorn, Bob Becking, and Pieter W. van der
               Horst. Leiden: Brill, 1995.
ErIsr   *Eretz-Israel*
HSM   Harvard Semitic Monographs
HSS   Harvard Semitic Studies
IDBSup   *Interpreter's Dictionary of the Bible: Supplementary Vol-
               ume.* Edited by Keith Crim. Nashville: Abingdon, 1976.
JAOS   *Journal of the American Oriental Society*
JBL   *Journal of Biblical Literature*
JCS   *Journal of Cuneiform Studies*
JEOL   *Jaarbericht van het Vooraziatisch-Egyptisch Gezelschap
               (Genootschap) Ex oriente lux*
JNES   *Journal of Near Eastern Studies*
JSOTSup   Journal for the Study of the Old Testament Supplement
               Series
LAPO   Littératures anciennes du Proche-Orient
MDOG   *Mitteilungen der Deutschen Orient-Gesellschaft*
NABU   *Nouvelles assyriologiques breves et utilitaires*
NCB   New Century Bible
OBO   Orbis biblicus et orientalis
OEANE   *The Oxford Encyclopedia of Archaeology in the Near East.*
               Edited by Eric M. Meyers. New York: Oxford University
               Press, 1997.
OIP   Oriental Institute Publications
OLA   Orientalia lovaniensia analecta
Or   *Orientalia* (NS)
OTL   Old Testament Library
PEQ   *Palestine Exploration Quarterly*
PSD   *The Sumerian Dictionary of the University Museum of the
               University of Pennsylvania.* Edited by Åke W. Sjöberg et al.
               Philadelphia: Babylonian Section of the University Museum,
               1984–.
RHR   *Revue de l'histoire des religions*
RIM   The Royal Inscriptions of Mesopotamia Project. Toronto
RIME   The Royal Inscriptions of Mesopotamia, Early Periods
RlA   *Reallexikon der Assyriologie und vorderasiatischen
               Archäologie.* Edited by Erich Ebeling et al. Berlin: de
               Gruyter, 1928–.
SBLWAW   Society of Biblical Literature Writings from the Ancient
               World

SSN	Studia semitica neerlandica
STDJ	Studies on the Texts of the Desert of Judah
TCS	Texts from Cuneiform Sources
TynBul	*Tyndale Bulletin*
VAB	Vorderasiatische Bibliothek
VT	*Vetus Testamentum*
VTSup	Supplements to Vetus Testamentum
YOS	Yale Oriental Series, Texts
ZA	*Zeitschrift für Assyriologie*

1
THE LAND AND ITS PEOPLE

Lo, I am bringing against you, O House of Israel,
a nation from afar—declares the LORD;
It is an enduring nation, It is an ancient nation;
A nation whose language you do not know—You will not understand
    what they say.

Jeremiah 5:15 (NJPS)

Who Were the Babylonians? The question evokes images of distant empires built along the Euphrates River and of mighty armies marauding through western Asia in preclassical history. For readers of the Bible, the question also arouses specific images of the seemingly all-powerful nation used by God to punish Israel, a nation that eventually came to represent in biblical imagery all that was evil. For students of ancient history generally, interest in the Babylonians stems from the nearly countless innovations and contributions of the Babylonians to preclassical Mesopotamian civilization. As we shall see, the Babylonians left a permanent mark on human history in literature, art, science, and religion.

This first chapter begins to address the question, *Who Were the Babylonians?* Here I will offer a general summary of their role in ancient history, describing the geographical features of their homeland in lower Mesopotamia, and detailing the chronological framework of their historical periods. The chapter closes with a section on the primary sources from the ancient world that tell us who the Babylonians were. Subsequent chapters detail the specifics of the general portrait presented here.

1.1. THE STAGE: THE GEOGRAPHY OF BABYLONIA

Ancient Babylonia was located in southern Mesopotamia, which itself constituted part of the ancient Near East. The phrase "ancient Near East(ern)" refers to the areas comprised today of Iran, Iraq, Kuwait, Saudia Arabia, Jordan, Turkey, Syria, Lebanon, Israel, Palestine, and Egypt. Here I summarize the geographical features of Mesopotamia, giving special attention to southern Mesopotamia, or "Babylonia."

The story of human civilization begins here, in the interconnected riverine cultures of Egypt and Mesopotamia. Together these valley civilizations form the matrix of ancient Near Eastern culture and the birthplace of human civilization. Yet Egypt is geographically very different from the Tigris-Euphrates valley. Throughout ancient Near Eastern history (approximately 4000–330 B.C.E.), Egypt was largely isolated from the rest of western Asia because it was limited to the narrow band of hospitable land created by the Nile Valley. As a result, Egypt was rarely impacted by intrusions from different nationalities, seldom exported its language or script, and retained its distinctive culture throughout most of its history. By contrast, Mesopotamia was open and vulnerable at nearly all borders and therefore was impacted by a steady infusion of different nationalities and people groups. Its distinctive cuneiform script was exported to all points of the compass and adapted to many languages.

I begin by clarifying the way I will use terms in this volume. Throughout this study I will follow the conventional practice of using "Babylonia" and "Babylonian(s)" for things related to the city of Babylon itself, as well as for the greater region of southern Mesopotamia in what is today southern Iraq, Kuwait, and parts of western Iran. However, this was not the practice of the ancients themselves. While the city name "Babylon" has a long and established history, the region itself has gone under a variety of names. In the third and early second millennia B.C.E., southern Mesopotamia was "Sumer" and central Mesopotamia was "Akkad."[1]

The city of Babylon itself was located along the Araḫtum, either a branch of the Euphrates or the Euphrates itself.[2] The city went by a variety of names in antiquity. The earliest form of "Babylon" appears to have been *babil(a)*, the origin and meaning of which are lost to antiquity.[3] The city's existence may be traced to the third millennium B.C.E., although it was relatively insignificant politically during that period (see ch. 2). Nonetheless, the name of the location "Babil(a)" was of neither Sumerian nor Akkadian origin and so perhaps derives ultimately from the population inhabiting Mesopotamia before the Sumerians, the so-called proto-Euphratean population.

This ancient and now obscure name for the city gave rise to an Akkadian form, created through popular etymology, *bāb-ilim,* "Gate of God," which then assumed a Sumerian equivalent, ka-dingirra, also meaning "Gate of God." Earlier scholarship assumed this Sumerian version was older and more original and that the Akkadian *bāb-ilim* was derivative. However, Ignace J. Gelb argued that the Akkadian preceded the Sumerian equivalent and was probably created by wordplay on the even older *babil(a)*.[4] It is currently impossible to determine which was primary. The later plural form, *bāb-ilāni,* "Gate of the Gods," became *babylôn* in Greek, resulting in the modern name "Babylon." Several literary names for the city, such as *tintirki,* probably became popular in the twelfth century B.C.E.[5] The Kassites of the Middle Babylonian period (ch. 4) knew the region as Kar-Duniash.[6]

The geographical extent of Babylonia varies, of course, depending on the particular historical period in question. In general, the Tigris and Euphrates rivers form an alluvial plain just south of modern Baghdad, where they flow closest to each other, extending southeastward to the marshes of the Persian Gulf. This plain constitutes the geographical heartland of Babylonia proper (see fig. 1.1).[7] Throughout much of ancient history, "Babylonia" was limited to this relatively small region of southern

Fig. 1.1. Water courses of southern Mesopotamia and the cities of the Early Dynastic periods. The Euphrates today flows west of most of the sites, while the Tigris is farther east (solid lines). Adapted from Robert McC. Adams, *The Evolution of Urban Society* (Chicago: Aldine, 1966), 70.

Mesopotamia, which has few clearly demarcated natural boundaries. The south is bounded by the Persian Gulf in the southeast and the Arabian Desert in the southwest. The Zagros Mountains and the Iranian plateau to the east of the Tigris serve generally to mark the eastern frontier. The Zagros Mountains also rise to the region's northeast, while the open alluvial plain of the rest of central Mesopotamia lies due north. The Syrian Desert alone defines the western frontier of Babylonia. Rainfall is limited in this alluvial plain, but agriculture is possible and often richly productive, using irrigation of water from the rivers. The southernmost part of Babylonia consists of marshes, where people have lived in villages of reed houses or on boats for thousands of years. In antiquity, inhabitants of the marshes lived in isolation during all but the most stable of political times, which often attracted individuals "on the run" for whatever reason.[8] Babylonia was a land poor in raw materials such as metals, stone, and wood, which were sometimes acquired through trade exchanging crafts, especially textiles and leatherwork.

Thus we may use "south Mesopotamia" to distinguish this riverine plain from the northern regions between the Zagros Mountains and the Euphrates River at Carchemish in the northwest, or "north Mesopotamia." Although north and south share the cultural features that justify the study of "ancient Mesopotamia," the climatic and geographical differences between them are also significant enough to distinguish Babylonia from Assyria.

For reasons that will likely always remain obscure, this area of southern Mesopotamia became the stage upon which humankind's grand drama was to begin—this is the site of the world's first urban civilization. Southern Mesopotamia jumped ahead of other regions of the ancient world in material culture and seldom lost its position of prominence until the time of Alexander the Great and the spread of Greek culture. There were no doubt many factors leading to this development, but the most important may have been access to water, which was critical for the development of the first villages and cities.[9] The Euphrates meanders about and flows slower than does the Tigris and therefore provides an easier resource for irrigation. Consequently, the oldest and most important cities of the region were located along the Euphrates and its many canals and tributaries. In the fourth millennium B.C.E., southern Mesopotamia witnessed an urban explosion, as can be demonstrated by archaeological surface surveys.[10] Traces of ancient branches of the Euphrates, which flowed through the alluvial plain, are still visible in the region north and east of Nippur, which was heavily populated and the site of many of the earliest villages in the early fourth millennium B.C.E. (see fig. 1.1). Later in that millennium, many of these sites were abandoned and new villages were established farther south near Uruk ("Erech" in the Bible [Gen 10:10] and "Warka" today).

Gradually small villages declined and larger centers developed in a slow process of urbanization. Although access to water was certainly crucial in this development, paradoxically the inhospitable terrain also contributed to the rise of human civilization in southern Mesopotamia. The growth of cities and loss of villages may be attributed to the need for community organization of labor for purposes of irrigation and cultivation. Thus, cultural and intellectual advances were made possible by the early Sumerian city-states. By the end of the fourth millennium B.C.E., Uruk had become what may be properly called a city, with large monumental public architecture, efflorescent art, the accumulation of capital, the production of the earliest written documents discovered to date, and foreign trade and commerce.[11] Thus historians call this "the Uruk period," which is variously subdivided into the Early Uruk period (ca. 3500–3200 B.C.E.) and the Late Uruk period (ca. 3200–2900 B.C.E.).[12]

This process of urbanization continued into the third millennium, when the region saw widespread prosperity at capital cities located along the rivers and canals at Kish, Nippur, Lagash, Uruk, Eridu, Shuruppak, and Ur, supported by a flourishing economy and an efficient system of irrigation.[13] During the fourth and third millennia B.C.E., the Euphrates did not flow through a single channel but probably had three primary branches, along which the most important cities were established (see fig. 1.1).[14] The city of Babylon itself was located beside a minor branch of the Euphrates to the west and was of little significance politically during this period. We have no evidence of its existence prior to the middle of the third millennium.

Throughout most of the historical periods covered in this book, "Babylonia" will be limited to this relatively small region of southern Mesopotamia. However, on the few occasions when certain rulers managed to build Babylonian empires, "Babylonia" may be said to have extended beyond these general boundaries, stretching out across the Fertile Crescent into Syria-Palestine and, indeed, most of western Asia. In the second millennium, Hammurapi built an empire with Babylon at its center, extending for the first time beyond southern Mesopotamia into the northwestern bend of the Euphrates river (ch. 3). Some of the Kassite rulers of the Middle Babylonian period were able to achieve nearly the same political boundaries (ch. 4). Much later, the empire of Nebuchadnezzar II again exceeded the traditional borders of Babylonia, although he shared the northern regions of western Asia with the Medes (ch. 6). Such expansive empires were normally short lived, and the Babylonians seldom controlled territory beyond southern Mesopotamia for prolonged periods of time.

As will become clear in the pages to follow, Babylonia's sociopolitical history is characterized by numerous invasions and hostile forces moving into the region, making its history a tapestry of disparate ethnic groups and successive cultural influences amalgamating into the whole. Babylonia was the "melting pot" of antiquity. This is due largely to the fact that the Babylonian heartland was vulnerable to invasion because of a severe lack of natural barriers in the physical landscape. In particular, the Euphrates corridor in the northwest was the scene for numerous invasions of seminomadic populations, most importantly the Amorites and Arameans, as we shall see. The marshes in the south offered no resistance to invaders from the plains of Persia or from the Persian Gulf itself. Invaders could also descend upon the urban centers of central Babylonia from the Zagros hills to the east and northeast.

1.2. THE PLAYERS: ETHNICITY AND THE IDENTITY OF THE BABYLONIANS

Having established the essential geographical data and boundaries of ancient Babylonia, it would appear to be a simple task to describe precisely *who* the Babylonians were. They may be described as the inhabitants of this location for nearly two millennia, from early in the second millennium B.C.E. until the Persian Empire. However, it is not entirely as simple as that. In contrast to the Egyptians with their relative isolation, the identity of the Babylonians is of necessity more complex because of the frequent infusion of ethnic groups from outside southern Mesopotamia. The periods in question are marked by an ebb and flow of disparate peoples and a resultant mixture of people groups. In sum, the Babylonians were generally Amorite and Kassite during the second millennium B.C.E.; in the first millennium, they were an amalgamation of these older groups—now the "native" Babylonians—with Arameans, Chaldeans, and many others.

In this book I have been rather traditional in periodizing Babylonia's history along lines of political developments, primarily giving pride of place to particular dynasties in power over certain periods of time. Thus I will focus primarily on the Old Babylonian Empire of Hammurapi, the Middle Babylonian Kassite rule, and the Neo-Babylonian Empire of Nebuchadnezzar II and his dynasty. This schema is desirable to some extent because it stands in a long line of history-writing related to the ancient Near East extending back to the nineteenth century; it will give the reader context for understanding ancient history generally; and it will make it easier to locate the ethnic identity of the "main players" of the Babylonian drama in particular. It should be kept in mind, however, that such facile periodization is almost arbitrary and, worse, misleading because it is based largely on philological criteria rather than historical ones. That is, our periods of history, and hence my chapter divisions, reflect royal dynasties and in some cases international empires with extensive textual remains (e.g., Neo-Sumerian period, Neo-Babylonian period), while those political entities with little textual remains are grouped together into a long period (such as the Middle Babylonian).[15] Moreover, this periodization also assumes the historical positivism of the nineteenth century and may lead us to miss certain social and economic continuities in the ancient world that can provide a more balanced portrait of everyday life in ancient Babylonia.[16] While the historical periodization is unavoidable and to a limited degree even desirable, we should not lose sight of its inadequacies especially for the less-attested periods and its tendency to obscure the degree of social and cultural continuity in Babylonian history.

On the other hand, the periodization most often used for the ancient Near East in general is not always very helpful. Archaeologists conventionally use a "three-age system" of stone, bronze, and iron devised originally by the Danish scholar Christian Thomsen in the early nineteenth century in order to classify the collection of the National Museum of Denmark.[17] Thomsen's schematization supposed that the three ages followed in order of increasingly advanced technology in the production of tools and weapons, using first stone, then bronze, and finally iron, in a linear evolution. The three-age system has been widely adopted and elaborated by subdivisions into Early, Middle, and Late Bronze Ages and three Iron ages as well as by the insertion of a Copper Age (Chalcolithic) between the Stone and Bronze ages (see fig. 1.2, where respective dates between Syria-Palestine and Southern Mesopotamia will be obvious). However, it is now widely acknowledged that the concept of linear evolution of cultures and societies at the base of this system was simplistic and no longer tenable and that the use of the three technological media was hardly restricted to their respective ages. Nonetheless, the terminology is so deeply established and practically useful that it is routinely in use, especially for describing history in the Levant and in Anatolia. In Mesopotamian studies, it is more customary to denote historical periods by "phases" or "cultures," named after geographical locations in the earlier periods (e.g., Ubaid, Early Uruk, Late Uruk periods) or sociopolitical developments (e.g., Early Dynastic periods, Old Akkadian period, Neo-Sumerian, Old Babylonian). I will use the "Bronze Age" and "Iron Age" designations only sparingly as a means of coordinating our story with that of the rest of ancient Near Eastern history.

The arrival of the Amorites into central and southern Mesopotamia constituted a turning point in ancient history. Indeed, a distinction may be made between the third and second millennia on the basis of their influence in the region.[18] In a sense, Babylonian civilization proper began in the early second millennium B.C.E., when the Amorite city-states of various sizes slowly supplanted the Sumero-Akkadian culture of the previous millennium. In particular, the first dynasty of Babylon was established by the Amorites in the nineteenth century B.C.E. and rose to prominence under its

Fig. 1.2. Comparative Archaeological Periods:
Syria-Palestine and Southern Mesopotamia

Syria-Palestine	*Southern Mesopotamia*
Paleolithic (before 14,000)	Paleolithic (before 20,000)
Epipaleolithic (14,000–8000)	Epipaleolithic (20,000–10,000)
Neolithic (8000–4200)	Neolithic (9000–5000)
	Samarra period (5000–4000)
Chalcolithic (4200–3300)	Ubaid period (4000–3500)
Early Bronze I (3300–3000)	Uruk period (3500–3200)
	Late Uruk/Jemdet Nasr period (3200–2900)
Early Bronze II (3000–2800)	Early Dynastic I (2900–2700) Early Dynastic II (2700–2600) Early Dynastic III (2600–2350)
Early Bronze III (2800–2400)	Old Akkadian period (2350–2193)
Early Bronze IV (2400–2000)	Neo-Sumerian period (2112–2004)
Middle Bronze Age I (2000–1800) Middle Bronze Age II (1800–1650) Middle Bronze Age III (1650–1550)	Old Babylonian period (2003–1595)
Late Bronze Age I (1550–1400) Late Bronze Age II (1400–1200)	Middle Babylonian period (1595–1155)
Iron I (1200–930) Iron IIA (930–721) Iron IIB (721–605) Iron IIC (605–539)	Early Neo-Babylonian period (1155–625) Neo-Babylonian period (625–539)
Persian (539–332)	Persian (539–332)

sixth ruler, Hammurapi (1792–1750 B.C.E.).[19] Scholars frequently refer to this period of history as the Old Babylonian period (2000–1595 B.C.E.; see ch. 3 below).

After Hammurapi's dynasty fell to the Hittites in 1595 B.C.E., the role of the Amorites began to wane, and the identity of the Babylonians changed dramatically. Kassite rulers took up governance of Babylonia for several centuries in what is most conveniently called the Middle Babylonian period (1595–1155 B.C.E.; see ch. 4 below). During this period the inhabitants of Babylonia were a mixture of ethnolinguistic groups, including Kassites, Assyrians, Elamites, Hurrians, precursors of the Arameans and Chaldeans, and others.

Toward the end of the second millennium and for several centuries in the first millennium B.C.E., Assyrian monarchs to the north strove to rule Babylon, which was by now venerated as the cultural capital of all Mesopotamia. Its political significance was often derived from this perception of Babylon as an ancient holy city, making it an important symbol of power and legitimacy for Assyrian kings. Meanwhile in Babylonia proper, "native" Babylonians (now an amalgamation of various ethnolinguistic groups) and newly settled Aramean and Chaldean tribes attempted to gain independence from the Assyrians in order to rule Babylonia themselves, in what may be called the Early Neo-Babylonian period (1155–625 B.C.E.; see ch. 5 below).

Eventually Nabopolassar (625–605 B.C.E.) and his son and successor Nebuchadnezzar II (604–562 B.C.E.) participated in the defeat of the Assyrians and restored Babylon to a brief period of renewed grandeur, in what is sometimes called the Chaldean Empire, or the Neo-Babylonian period (625–539 B.C.E.; see ch. 6). With the rise of Cyrus, Babylon became a province in the expansive Persian Empire and was eventually taken by Alexander the Great and his successors. During the Hellenistic period, Babylon eventually lost its cultural and political supremacy to Seleucia on the Tigris.

1.3. SIGNIFICANCE OF THE BABYLONIANS FOR HISTORY AND BIBLICAL STUDIES

Historians and biblical scholars study the Babylonians for numerous reasons. We turn now to consider first the significance of the Babylonians in ancient Near Eastern history generally, then their significance for biblical studies in particular.

The Babylonians, together with their predecessors in the third millennium B.C.E., the Sumerians, may be credited with establishing the ideological and social infrastructure for ancient Mesopotamian culture. The Babylonians inherited from the Sumerians many cultural and religious features, which they preserved and transmitted throughout much of western Asia. Other essential components of the Mesopotamian cultural heritage were Babylonian innovations. It is difficult to overestimate the significance of these Babylonian contributions to ancient Mesopotamian society and culture.

The comprehensive significance of ancient Babylonia is often underestimated because we tend to embrace the influence on contemporary human civilization of later ancient societies and their literary accomplishments, such as those of Israel, Greece, and Rome.[20] But those important cultures were part of a larger continuum in the ancient world, for which the Babylonians were important innovators. Moreover, because of Babylonia's rich textual resources, we know more about their ancient society than we do of Egypt and other areas of the ancient world, making a study of the ancient Babylonians particularly fruitful for history generally.

More particularly, the role of the Babylonians in the Bible is interesting, especially in light of the pejorative tone adopted so frequently by authors of the Hebrew Scriptures when referring to them. Counting references in both the Hebrew Scriptures and the Christian New Testament, the Bible mentions Babylon, the region of Babylonia, or its inhabitants over four hundred times in a variety of ways. In addition, the ethnicon, *kaśdîm*, "Chaldea/n/s," occurs ninety times, and the eight occurrences of the appellation *šin'ār*, "Shinar" appear to denote southern Mesopotamia generally. Because of its international and cultural significance in the early periods, and its role later in destroying Jerusalem and deporting large portions of its citizens, Babylon came to carry theological significance in the Bible as well as its obvious historical importance. Jeremiah's description quoted at the heading of this chapter is typical. The nation used as an instrument of divine wrath is a distant one of strange and incomprehensible speech, a distant and foreign nation of long duration. Such a frightening nation could also be referred to by the ancient literary technique known as *atbash*, in which "Sheshach" is a cryptogram for "Babylon" in contexts of rebellion and horror, and "Leb-qamai" stands for "Chaldea" (Jer 25:26; 51:41; Jer 51:1, respectively).[21] From the perspective of the Israelite prophet, Babylon may be compared to Sheol, for just as Sheol's appetite for the dead is insatiable, so is the greed of the Babylonian Empire for other nations (Hab 2:5).

The question, then, *Who Were the Babylonians?* is important for students and scholars of the Bible, first because of the fascinating but complex problem of the literary relationship between the creation stories of Genesis and the Babylonian Epic of Creation (Akkadian title *Enūma Eliš;* see ch. 5) or the relationship of the Bible's flood narrative in Gen 6–9 and the eleventh tablet of the Gilgamesh Epic as well as the Epic of Atraḥasis (ch. 3). To these intriguing literary parallels may be added the much later traditions about the Babylonian royal court preserved in the book of Daniel.

A second reason students of the Bible seek to understand more about the ancient Babylonians is because of the many references in the historical books of the Hebrew Bible especially to events in which Babylon plays a central role. Names of Babylonians such as Merodach-baladan, Nebuchadnezzar, Evil-merodach, Nebuzaradan, and others, once only dimly perceived via the Hellenistic sources, are now attested in native Babylonian sources and contribute considerably to our understanding of the Hebrew narratives. Beyond such specifics, the retrieval of native Babylonian sources in the past 150 years has made it possible to reconstruct in part the broad sociopolitical history of ancient Babylonia presented in these pages, and it is imperative that students and scholars of the Bible's historical books become familiar with this history generally, especially the Neo-Babylonian Empire (ch. 6).

A third reason students of the Bible are interested in the Babylonians is related to the way the Bible perceives and scrutinizes Babylonian ideology, specifically Babylonian religion and imperialism as it is critiqued by the Hebrew prophetic literature.[22] Here Babylon consistently comes to symbolize an evil power, although at times Yhwh (Israel's God, Yahweh, "the LORD" of most translations) used evil Babylonia to accomplish a wider purpose. In Jeremiah, Babylonia is cryptically denoted when Yhwh warns that disaster will break forth "out of the north" (1:14 and 6:1, 22–23). But ultimately the prophet is comforted by the knowledge that Babylon will one day encounter its own enemy from the north, when Medo-Persian forces will come upon it for destruction (50:41–42). The downfall of the king of Babylon is celebrated in Isa 14:4–23 in terms that came to symbolize the destruction of any hostile enemy of God. In Second Isaiah (Isa 40–55), Babylon is a symbol of the evil oppressor. In Isa 47 Babylon is described as a beautiful woman reduced to slavery (47:1): "Come down and sit in the dust, virgin daughter Babylon! Sit on the ground without a throne, daughter Chaldea!" The long-awaited return from exile in Babylonia is described as a miraculous event comparable to the crossing of the Red Sea (Isa 51:9–11). The role of Babylon in Dan 1–5 is that of a ferocious human empire capable of many atrocities, yet vulnerable and ultimately doomed because of God's opposition. Belshazzar's writing on the wall illustrates the outcome of obstinate royal opposition to God's will (Dan 5). In many poetic passages, Babylon came to represent the place of exile and alienation: "By the rivers of Babylon—there we sat down and there we wept" (Ps 137:1).

The historical and political realities of the Iron Age led Israelite authors to characterize Babylonia as the place of religious hubris and degrading idolatry, tantamount to a refusal to worship or acknowledge the rightful place of deity. So in the New Testament, Babylon continued to symbolize avaricious power, the evil influences of sin and idolatry, and all anti-God predilections. The derogatory reference to "Babylon" in 1 Pet 5:13 is probably an allusion to the pretensions of Rome. In the book of Revelation references to Babylon become especially vitriolic, probably revealing again that Babylon is a cipher for Rome. Babylon is portrayed as the great prostitute seated on many waters, representing the various nationalities that Babylon subjugated (17:1, 15). She is "Babylon the great, mother of whores and of earth's abominations" (17:5). Because of her great pride and luxurious living at the expense of those she tormented, Babylon's downfall is swift and total: "For in one hour your judgment has come" (18:10; see also 18:17, 19).

At times this interest of biblical scholars in Assyriology (or the study of ancient Mesopotamia) has sparked debate. At the turn of the twentieth century, when large quantities of new information from ancient Assyria and Babylonia began to fuel intense interest, scholars were intrigued with parallels in biblical literature. At first most scholars assumed the primacy of Israelite ideas at the expense of the Babylonians. But eventually this gave way to the rise of "pan-Babylonianism" and one of the most spectacular debates of the early twentieth century, embroiling leading scholars of Europe and even involving the German emperor, Kaiser Wilhelm II.[23] Such pan-Babylonianism assumed that all creative and innovative ideas originated in Babylonia, moving westward to be recycled and diluted by the Israelites. These views were often intertwined with political convictions in central Europe and at times were fueled by racism and anti-Semitic motives. Although this approach has long since been abandoned in favor of a more balanced comparative-contrastive approach, some scholars continue to err, either in neglecting ancient Near Eastern studies altogether or in over-emphasizing the conceptual and cultural continuum between Mesopotamia and Israel. A balanced approach must begin by recognizing that Israel and its neighbors shared a common culture, from which each one differed to varying degrees. The similarities between Israel and Babylonia have been well documented: the religiously dominated culture vis-à-vis today's secularizing materialism, the principle of association that governed intellectual processes, and the basic conservatism of both civilizations. Similarities such as these only serve to make the disparities more informative and hence justify a careful comparative method that reconstructs the context or horizontal dimensions of a text (i.e., its geographical, historical, religious, political, and literary setting).[24]

1.4. SOURCES FOR THE STUDY OF THE BABYLONIANS

In many ways the study of the ancient Babylonians is a relatively new discipline when compared to biblical studies or other topics in the humanities. Archaeology uncovered and retrieved the ancient societies of

Mesopotamia only during the past 150 years.[25] Prior to the discovery of ancient Assyria and Babylonia in the mid-nineteenth century and the subsequent decipherment of their texts, the only sources available for the Babylonians were the Bible and the Greek historians.

Of the Greek historians, the predecessors of Herodotus are poorly preserved and were interested for the most part in Assyria more than Babylonia.[26] Herodotus, on the other hand, recorded an impressive description of the city of Babylon, which has been largely confirmed by modern archaeologists. His assessment of Babylonian customs (e.g., marriage practices, death rituals, religious beliefs) has not met with equal appreciation, which probably reflects the tendency among Greek historians to judge foreign customs as inferior to Greek civilization at the time. Likewise, his sketch of Babylonian history has raised questions. He considers an Assyrian queen, Semiramis, to be the builder of Babylon, and he also refers to two Babylonian kings, both known as Labynetus, and a queen, Nitokris. The identity of these figures has been the subject of much scholarly attention, but at present there is no consensus that matches them to historically attested Babylonian personages.[27] Berossus, a third-century B.C.E. priest of Marduk, wrote *Babyloniaca* at the request of the Seleucid king Antiochus I. This work—again known only in fragments—was a three-volume history of Babylonia that apparently relied on Babylonian historical traditions and chronicles.[28] Few historical specifics can be gleaned from these sources, although they perpetuated for the ages the perception of Babylonia as an ancient center of learning and culture.

With the retrieval of ancient preclassical societies through archaeological excavation over the past 150 years, we also retrieved thousands of written sources restoring the voices of the Babylonians themselves to illuminate their history.

> One of the most characteristic features of the archeology of Mesopotamia is the abundance of texts written, for the most part, on unbaked clay tablets. Half a million cuneiform tablets have been recovered from archeological sites in the Near East, many of which have not yet been published. Many more tablets are still buried under the ground.[29]

The cuneiform system of writing is a script, not a language. It lent itself easily to various occasions, as the need arose, which in turn means we have recovered a variety of text types. For economic and legal transactions, clay tablets were deposited in *archival* collections that were expected to last for a few generations only. For more permanent records or for text intended for public display, inscriptions were written on monuments of stone (such as Hammurapi's famous law code) and may therefore be considered *monumental*. The Babylonian belles-lettres (or literary texts) were preserved by repeated copying in scribal schools, particularly in the Old

Babylonian period and by royal and temple scholars of the first millennium B.C.E., and have thus been called *canonical* texts.[30]

In Babylonia, a "stream of tradition" (to use Oppenheim's terminology) or literary "canon" was probably established around 1200 B.C.E.[31] Although "canon" has become a convenient way of referring to this collection of text types—and one that has the advantage of communicating a common

Fig. 1.3. Babylonian Map of the world.
Babylon is the rectangle at the center with the Euphrates flowing
through it. Distant localities are shown beyond the concentric circles.
© Copyright The British Museum.

ground between Western readers familiar with the Bible and these ancient texts—perhaps "scribal curriculum" would be better.[32] Many of the literary pieces we would identify as belles-lettres are preserved in late copies only, known to us primarily from royal or scribal libraries in a single Standard Babylonian corpus. Many of the literary texts certainly go back to earlier periods in their originals, such as the Old Babylonian period, for example. In addition, there are a few copies of literary texts from earlier periods that, for whatever reason, were not included in the scribal curriculum. In this case, the literary text served a "canonical" function in the earlier historical period but did not become part of the first-millennium scribal curriculum.

We are seldom able to date Akkadian literary compositions on the basis of style or language, and therefore it is often impossible to determine when one of these literary texts was first composed. Nevertheless, I have chosen to arrange this volume according to Babylonia's sociopolitical history and to introduce and discuss certain of these literary creations in the most likely period of their composition, making some of the discussion tentative at best.

Fortunately, the ancient Babylonians established scholarly academies for the purpose of training scribes to take administrative positions in palaces or temples, and these scribes copied and preserved scientific scholarly works and the literature of the past. In some cases, collections were housed in private residences by individual families, but often in temples and palaces. Although the concept of "library" is more of a first-millennium one, we know that in Babylonia proper a scribal academy existed at Nippur as early as the Neo-Sumerian period, where texts were collated, copied, or even composed, preserving many Old Sumerian literary works. The accidents of catastrophic destruction and recovery have left large collections of tablets we might not otherwise have. So, for example, the enormous stash of tablets from the end of the Neo-Sumerian period are the result of the sudden burial of its leading cities at the hands of the Elamites in 2004 B.C.E. Likewise, the end of the Old Babylonian period left large libraries at Sippar and Larsa.[33] The idea of archiving texts was exported to the Assyrians, who were known to have had a library at Ashur as early as Tiglath-Pileser I (1115–1077 B.C.E.), and we have evidence to suggest he was preceded by Ashur-uballit I (1363–1328).[34] In later Assyrian times, libraries were known to have existed at the temples of Nabû, the Babylonian scribal god and patron of writing, in Neo-Assyrian capitals: Nineveh, Nimrud, and Dur-Sharrukin. Nineveh has also produced, famously, two royal libraries in northwest and southwest palaces of the ancient city, and much of what we know today of Assyrian and Babylonian history and culture comes from these libraries. Ashurbanipal (668–627 B.C.E.) issued orders to his agents in the south to collect every single tablet in their areas, especially all library collections (called "Ezida" after the name of Nabû's temple in Borsippa), which held a variety of text types, all of which were desirable to Ashurbanipal.[35] A small Neo-Babylonian library was discovered at ancient Sippar in 1986 filled with literary texts "copied from originals" from Babylon, Nippur, Akkad, and other places, confirming the range of compositions known from other collections.[36]

Most of these tablet collections were not literary in nature but rather more like scientific or scholarly reference works, such as omen texts, lexical lists like ancient dictionaries, incantations, and religious texts such as prayers. If Ashurbanipal's library was representative of such library collections, and we have every reason to believe it was, then most of the texts in these collections were not examples of ancient Babylonian belles-lettres at all, even though today's scholars persist in calling them that. Rather, true literary texts were a fraction of what has been preserved.[37]

The categories of native Babylonian sources used in this volume will include administrative and economic documents, legal documents, letters, historiographic texts, literary texts, and scholarly texts.[38] The chapters devoted to the Old and Neo-Babylonian periods will be largely dependent upon King Lists and chronographic materials, making it possible to reconstruct in outline the sociopolitical events of those periods. Royal inscriptions of a variety of types will obviously be important, especially for the first empires of the Early Bronze Age, the Old Babylonian Empire, and the Neo-Babylonian kings. In chapter 3 the use of legal materials, especially Hammurapi's legal collection, will receive much attention. The latter, along with literary compositions, such as the the Gilgamesh Epic, the Epic of Atra-ḫasis, and the *Enūma Eliš,* are of primary interest to students of the Bible. Finally, epistolary evidence is important in many periods, but especially in the Old Babylonian period.

2

BABYLONIA BEFORE THE BABYLONIANS:
THE THIRD MILLENNIUM B.C.E.

Prior to the emergence of Greece and Rome, the greatest advances of human civilization were in the ancient Near East. In Egypt and Mesopotamia, agriculture first evolved, and subsequently the region saw advances in urbanism, the invention of writing, the first metalworking, and eventually the first empires. During the earliest historical periods, more than five thousand years ago, human civilization emerged in this region, with all the complex social organizations—cities, societal structures, religion, and writing—that constitute the features of modern civilization as we know it. This chapter covers these developments in Babylonia prior to the rise of Babylon itself.

2.1. THE FIRST HISTORICAL PERIODS OF BABYLONIA

Several years ago a leading scholar of ancient Mesopotamia asserted in a book title that "history begins at Sumer."[1] Such an assertion has merit for a number of reasons, primarily because of the appearance of writing first in Sumer, or southern Babylonia. Since we are dependent upon written artifacts for the specifics of history (i.e., names of individuals and socio-political events), anything before that must of necessity be identified as "prehistoric," and thus history begins with writing.

Many of the features of human civilization appeared in southern Mesopotamia just prior to the invention of writing. It is the convergence of a number of innovations during the fourth millennium B.C.E.—the development of cities and urban architecture, the introduction of metallurgy, the flourishing of various art forms, the development of trade and commerce, the first use of the wheel, and so forth—that mark it as a transition from prehistory to history. As these features converged toward the conclusion of the fourth millennium B.C.E., the invention of writing appears among them, as illustrated best by the city of Uruk in what may be called the "Late Uruk period" (ca. 3200–2900 B.C.E., see previous chapter).[2] Rather than a single Sumerian innovation at Uruk, it is likely that the invention of writing was

17

a gradual process occurring across a wider region, including apparently ancient Elam to the east of Sumer (modern Iran).[3] Nevertheless, Uruk remains the best example of the process,[4] and the first identifiable language represented in syllabic cuneiform a century or more later is Sumerian. History, in fact, *does* begin at Sumer in ancient Babylonia.

The five or six centuries between the Late Uruk period and the rise of the first empires of Babylonia may be called the Early Dynastic period (ca. 2900–2350 B.C.E.) due to the emergence of various dynastic monarchies among the city-states of southern Mesopotamia. The specific chronology of individual dynasts is impossible to determine, and our dates for this period are tentative.[5] Scholars have subdivided this period into three phases as follows.[6]

Early Dynastic I (ca. 2900–2700)
Early Dynastic II (ca. 2700–2600)
Early Dynastic III (ca. 2600–2350)

The specifics of the sociopolitical history of this period are still poorly known, and we can only make several broad conclusions. We have various written sources from the period in the Sumerian language, which is still today obscure in some details. Most of these inscriptions are dedicatory foundation texts on bricks and door-hinge sockets, votive inscriptions on vases or mace heads, and, later on (particularly in ED III), economic and administrative inscriptions. These inscriptions shed light on the period, especially when combined with certain later literary texts. So, for example, scribal schools of the Old Babylonian period (ca. 1800 B.C.E.) preserved Sumerian Temple Hymns that claim to have been written by Enḫeduanna, a royal princess of the Old Akkadian Dynasty (and therefore from ca. 2300 B.C.E.; see below). The text is a collection of addresses to all the major sanctuaries of the Babylonia of that time, describing each temple and its deity.[7] Thus the Temple Hymns reveal what the most important cities were and the deities they worshiped in their temples.

In addition, the Sumerian King List remains an important source for this period, although it presents several problems for use as a source for history.[8] The King List preserves the names of 140 rulers who allegedly ruled over southern Mesopotamia. Its preamble describes the history of "kingship" (nam.lugal) from the moment it was lowered from heaven until the time of a great flood that swept over the earth, serving as a turning point in Mesopotamian history.[9] Rulers from this antediluvian period are said to have lived for extraordinarily long periods of time: eight rulers from five cities ruling for a total of 241,000 years. The rest of the text lists kings by their dynasties under the assumption that only one city served as the seat of kingship at a time, supposing that rulers from certain cities rose to power over others in a sort of revolving hegemony. The King List was likely compiled later (probably ca. 1800 B.C.E.) and contains obviously fanciful portraits (e.g., the impossibly long-lived antediluvian kings), and its nature as a "list" is inadequate to portray the political complexity of the period, since some of the kings were no doubt contemporaries. On the other hand, most agree that a genuine historical tradition is embedded in the Sumerian King List, and it may be supplemented with contemporary texts from the period to be used judiciously in reconstructing what we know of Babylonia's Early Dynastic period.

During this period Babylonia was governed by over thirty city-states.[10] The most important of these cities appear to be Eridu, Uruk, Umma, Lagash, Nippur, Ur, Kish, and Adab (see fig. 2.1). Each small state was centered on a capital city with its own patron deity and temple as well as, generally, a city ruler, whose title and ideology varied from city to city.[11] Most were called an ensi, "ruler, steward"; a few were en, "lord, dignitary" (such as at Uruk), or sanga, "chief temple administrator" (such as at Umma and Isin). Whatever the nomenclature, these secular rulers were intimately integrated into the cult of each city's patron deity, as the close association of these titles to temple authority makes clear (especially true for sanga

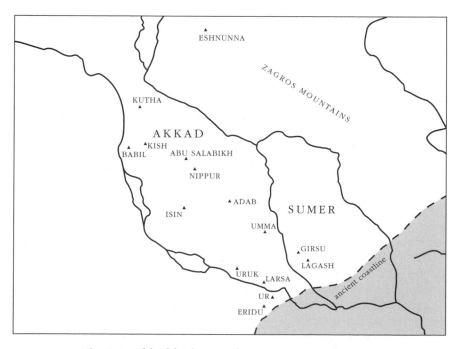

Fig. 2.1. Old Akkadian and Neo-Sumerian Periods.

and en). Even when the title lugal, "king," is used for secular domination of one state by another (especially at Kish; see below), it typically represents a nominal overlordship, which allowed the local ensi to retain the title and some degree of authority. These cities seemed to have shared a common cultural entity, embracing a conscious belonging to "The Land" (kalam), for which Nippur and its temple, Enlil, acted as the symbolic center. The cities appear to have collaborated for political and economic ventures and at times engaged in military attempts to dominate one another, as the appearance of fortification walls around some cities illustrates (ED II, ca. 2700 B.C.E.). No single city was able to impose lasting control of the others. Each appears to have valued its independence fervently.

Politically we have evidence of something like a "primitive democracy" for these city-states. The word for "king" (lugal) does not occur in the texts from the preceding Uruk or Jemdet Nasr periods, but the word for a local assembly of elder men (ukkin) certainly did. The rise of kingship was a gradual process in Early Dynastic times, despite the claims of the King List that it descended from heaven. In Babylonian myths from later times, deities were portrayed in assemblies reaching community decisions by consensus, and it seems reasonable to assume that this model had historical antecedents in the city-states of Early Dynastic times.[12] The value these cities placed on local autonomy appears to have resulted in a system that assigned responsibility to a city assembly comprised of all free males, perhaps superintended by the elders. It is also possible the city-states formed a sort of political league around their shared reverence for the god Enlil, chief of the pantheon, and for his temple Ekur at Nippur. If so, Nippur may also have been a place of assembly for league members to agree on mutually beneficial arrangements for trade and commerce.[13]

Each city's temple served as an important economic center and held considerable power (to a lesser degree, even true in the Late Uruk and Jemdet Nasr periods), establishing an important feature of Babylonian culture. Generally, this will be true of temples throughout Babylonian history, which unlike today's churches and synagogues were central factors in the society and economy of the urban communities.[14] Most temples controlled substantial wealth in the form of vast stores of grain harvested from the tracts of arable land under their control and were also the beneficiaries of both royal and private donations. Large numbers of workers (priestly and secular) owed their livelihood to the temples, some of which also used conscripted laborers for specific times of harvesting or irrigation. At one time scholars thought Early Dynastic Sumerian city-states were theocracies, or "temple states," meaning the deity was perceived as sole landowner and his or her temple wielded exclusive control of all land and labor. In recent decades, however, it has become clear that some land was privately owned and lay outside the control of the temple.[15] Indeed, as the city-state kings (whether actually called lugal, "king," ensi, "ruler, steward," or en, "lord") increased in power, they sometimes controlled the city's economy through intermediaries of large domains connected with the temple, and eventually the relationship between the secular ruler and the temple authority erupted in conflict. With the rise of the imperial might after this period, the relationship between temple and palace will change, as we shall see.

In Sumerian social structure generally, the nuclear family was the foundational unit, there being distinct designations for each parent and unmarried children of both genders, although Sumerian has a shortage of terms for collateral relatives (cousin, nephew, and niece). Unlike the kinship units and lineages of Semitic cultures of the early second millennium B.C.E., we have little evidence of anything like tribal lineages or extended kin units in the Early Dynastic period.[16]

The city of Kish had special political significance throughout the Early Dynastic period, and we have both textual and archaeological evidence that it rose to a quasi-hegemony over Sumer in ED III.[17] The traditions preserved in the King List confirm this view by listing Kish as the first holder of "kingship" after the flood, and the city's prestige as the preeminent seat of authority throughout the region led later Mesopotamian kings to assume the title "king of Kish" (šar kiššati).[18] Also toward the end of the Early Dynastic period, we learn more about one particularly important city, due partly to an accident of archaeology. Over sixteen hundred economic and administrative texts from Lagash and its capital Girsu, together with royal inscriptions from the city governors, give us the first real portrait of life during this period. We have details for as many as nine monarchs from Lagash during ED III, culminating in the last Early Dynastic king of Lagash, Uruinimgina (or Uru-kagina),[19] the great reformer, who is the first example of royal intervention in the law and the first Mesopotamian king to take actions to care for the orphan and the widow, which becomes a constant in Babylonian history.[20] His Reform Texts attempted to reform the laws in current practice in Sumerian culture, particularly by limiting bureaucracy and cutting taxes for the general populace. His attempt to standardize a legal system for ancient Babylonia would be a lasting legacy.

Before leaving the Early Dynastic period, a word is in order about Gilgamesh, fifth king of the first dynasty of Uruk according to the Sumerian King List and the hero of Babylonia's greatest literary work (see ch. 3). More stories were told of Gilgamesh than any other king of Babylonian history.[21] Although Gilgamesh is a legendary figure in this extensive epical literature, there are indications that he was a historical figure. We have discovered fragments of a royal inscription bearing the name En-mebaragesi, who was father of Gilgamesh's opponent, Akka of Kish.[22] In addition, we have a contemporary report of his having repaired a temple in Nippur.[23] These texts are only indirect confirmation of his existence, and his legendary status in the literature no doubt bears little resemblance to reality, but we should probably assume Gilgamesh was historical. The name Gilgamesh may itself have been a later epithet for the hero of legend, making it unlikely we will ever find the historical Gilgamesh.[24]

2.2. The First Empires of Babylonia

I have referred thus far to Sumerian culture and Sumerian city-states in the Early Dynastic period. But the populace of Babylonia was hardly homogeneous ethnically. We have reason to believe that the northern part of Babylonia throughout most of the Early Dynastic period was populated largely by Semites. Individuals bearing Semitic personal names appear in Sumerian texts from ancient Shuruppak by the middle of the third millennium B.C.E., and a surprisingly large number of scribes responsible for early Sumerian literary texts bear Semitic personal names at Abu Salabikh at about the same time.[25] Even the Sumerian King List is helpful here, because some of the personal names of kings who ruled Sumeria after the great flood are Semitic.

Of course, the presence of distinctive Semitic personal names is no guarantee of ethnic identification. It *does,* however, show evidence of the presence of Semitic speakers and demonstrates that at least a Semitic language substratum is present in Sumeria from earliest recorded times. We also have related evidence from an unlikely location. Far to the northwest at the ancient city of Ebla (modern Tell Mardikh) in northern Syria, archaeologists were startled in 1975 to discover an impressive and large archive of cuneiform tablets dated to the close of the Early Dynastic period. The archive, containing mostly administrative texts, was written in a mixture of Sumerian and Semitic, known today simply as "Eblaite." Some scholars have drawn connections between this Early Dynastic Semitic dialect and that of southern Mesopotamia, while others have discerned linguistic affiliations with the Old Assyrian dialect in northern Mesopotamia.[26] Since it predates the Old Akkadian period, it is better to refer to it simply as Old Semitic or Early Semitic rather than Akkadian. All these data suggest that southern Mesopotamia contained a significant Semitic element in the Early Dynastic period and perhaps earlier, and these Semites were integrated in the life of the cities, even serving as scribes in some cases, rather than nomadic tribesmen on the fringes of the culture.

As noted in chapter 1, Babylonia has few natural geographical boundaries. Additionally, the topographical details break the countryside naturally into north and south, so that by ED II enough Semites appear to have settled in the north to create a contrast between the Semitic north and the Sumerian south.[27] Sumerian was a living language in the third millennium B.C.E. and continued as a literary language (as a revered scholastic language, much like medieval Latin) in Old Babylonian schools (ca. 1600 B.C.E.) and to a lesser degree even into first century B.C.E.[28] The Semitic language of the Early Dynastic period is properly called Old Semitic, as we have seen, because of the discovery of Eblaite. More generally, it has come to be known as "Akkadian," following the example of the ancient Semitic-speaking Babylonians themselves, who derived the term from the city of Akkad (variously spelled Agade, Accad, or Akkade), built around 2300 B.C.E. by King Sargon I (*Akkadûm, AHw* 29, *CAD* A1, 272–73). Also known as East Semitic to distinguish it geographically from the Semitic languages of Arabia and Syria-Palestine to the west (e.g., Ugaritic, Canaanite, Aramaic, Hebrew), Akkadian was used extensively for nearly two millennia throughout Mesopotamia and even beyond it. The language is thus known to us in various dialects, most notably the Assyrian and Babylonian dialects of the second and first millennia, and unlike Sumerian is well understood by modern scholars.[29]

The relationship between the Sumerian and Akkadian languages during most of the third millennium reflects a long-standing division between the mainly Sumerian-speaking south and the predominantly Semitic-speaking north, especially around Kish and later Akkad.[30] Babylonia was called "Sumer and Akkad" during this period, and although speakers from north and south were often peacefully integrated in both regions, there was nonetheless a clear linguistic and ethnic north-south axis in the country. This important cultural feature plays a role in the development of Babylonia's first empire, that of the Akkadians.

2.2.1. OLD AKKADIAN PERIOD

North and south appear to have been unified politically under the strong leadership of Sargon I of Akkad around 2300 B.C.E. As conqueror and administrator, Sargon ushered in changes that resulted in a new phase of Babylonian history. He established a new capital at Akkad in the north, the specific location of which is still unknown, although most assume it was in the environs of modern Baghdad. Gradually the authority of the local ensis in the city-states was replaced by Akkadian governors loyal to a central administration at Akkad, and the independence of the long-revered city-states of Sumer in the south was abolished. Sargon himself claims that he defeated the major southern cities, destroyed their walls, and installed "sons of Akkad" as their ensis.[31] These profound innovations, and indeed the steps by which Sargon rose to strength, may be conjectured by means of analysis of his use of titles. He assumed the use of "King of Akkad" as he began subduing the city-states of the south, after which he became "King of the Land." It appears that Sargon then turned his expansionistic aspirations both to the east and northwest. Successful campaigns in Syria-Palestine and Elam may have been little more than military raids, but

Sargon apparently gained brief control of trade routes and collected tribute and from this point became "King of Kish." Ironically, the latter title
made it possible for Sargon to show respect for the Sumerian traditions,
retaining the prestige of the older tradition of hegemony throughout Sumer
and Akkad, while also introducing sweeping changes.[32]

The Old Akkadian language began to be used for royal inscriptions,
archives, and administrative texts, and the tablets themselves took on a
more rectangular form. The new centralized administration resulted in
Akkadian archives in distant locations, including Susa in the east, Gasur in
the northeast, and Tell Brak in the northwest corner of the upper
Euphrates.[33] A new unit of large-capacity measure (the so-called king's *gur*)
unified and replaced older cumbersome systems of calculation and transformed liquid and dry capacity measurements in Babylonia.[34]

Religiously, certain Semitic deities were elevated to new positions in
the pantheon; this was especially true for Semitic Ishtar, who was associated with Sumerian Inanna. Of note here is Sargon's daughter
Enheduanna, whom he installed as high priestess of the moon god Nanna
at Ur. Gifted with remarkable literary ability, Enheduanna is the first poet
in history known by name. She is credited with three separate poems in
Sumerian: the Temple Hymns (referred to earlier), a hymn to the goddess
Inanna, and the autobiographical hymn known as the Exaltation of
Inanna.[35] These hymns contain certain literary features that appear to
reflect an intentional effort to equate Ishtar with Inanna, setting the course
for a nearly complete syncretism between Sumerian and Semitic cultures
for centuries to come.

Sargon was followed in succession by two sons, Rimush and Manishtushu, who were largely occupied with repeated revolts in the south and
elsewhere (see fig. 2.2). It was his grandson, Naram-Sin, son of Manishtushu, who is often credited with transforming the realm he inherited into
a genuine empire, although the debate continues on whether we may
speak unequivocally of an "Akkadian Empire."[36] Naram-Sin conducted
military campaigns on all fronts: Syria, Anatolia, Elam, but above all, in the
south. A coalition of Sumerian city-states represented serious opposition,
but Naram-Sin claimed to have defeated the coalition quickly and decisively. Apparently in the wake of these military successes, Naram-Sin's
reign became the occasion for more innovations in the royal titulary. To
the titles used by his grandfather, Naram-Sin added "King of the Four
Quarters," apparently emphasizing the boundless nature of his empire.[37]
He also became the first king in recorded history in Babylonia to become
"god" of his city (a process known as "apotheosis," whereby someone is
deified). Whereas Egyptian pharaohs were routinely considered divine, at
least in part, the custom is rare among Babylonian kings. Naram-Sin
claimed the citizens of Akkad themselves asked the leading gods to make

Fig. 2.2. Dynasty of Akkad (Agade), 2350–2193

Sargon, 2334–2279
Rimush, 2278–2270
Manishtushu, 2269–2255
Naram-Sin, 2254–2218
Shar-kali-sharri, 2217–2193

---

their beloved king the protective deity of Akkad, and they built a temple for him in the midst of the city.[38] Scribes began using the determinative sign for deities (*dingir*) before Naram-Sin's name. His new status was represented iconographically by appearance of a royal horned tiara, which had been reserved for deities. His servants frequently addressed Naram-Sin as "the god of Akkad."[39] As such, he became owner of the city, and a few inscriptions even have Ishtar as his consort.

Although this phenomenon is poorly understood, it may have originated in the need to provide a patron deity for the city of Akkad and the Akkadian Empire generally. Given the assumptions of Babylonian philosophy, the "metaphor of divine favor" became central as a means of explaining the monarchy. That is, heaven and earth were intimately linked—events on earth mirrored those of heaven—resulting in a relationship between the Babylonian pantheon and human sociopolitical events. Perhaps the absence of a clear secular explanation for why one man should rise to authority over others resulted in the use of divine sanction as the explanation for otherwise inexplicable new historical circumstances.[40] Furthermore, unlike Nippur and other ancient cities in the south, Akkad appears to have had only a loose association with Ishtar, but no official patron deity. Perhaps the expansionistic innovations of the new empire required radical religious innovations as well, so the king served a new function in the capacity of deity, providing additional explanations for the many natural and social changes in the new order. Whatever the motives and origins, this divinizing feature of Babylonian kingship was continued by only a few subsequent kings and failed to take root as a fundamental characteristic of Babylonian kingship.

Ironically, during Naram-Sin's lifetime the end of Akkadian greatness was in sight. A combination of internal disruption, opposition from the Elamites in the east, and the arrival of Gutian tribesmen from the Zagros Mountains on the Iranian border resulted in a grossly weakened structure. It is likely that the role of the Gutians in the fall of Akkad has been overstated due to later Babylonian traditions and that they simply filled a power vacuum in an already weakened empire. Naram-Sin's son and successor, Shar-kali-sharri, relinquished the title "King of the Four Quarters,"

being simply "King of Akkad" instead. A string of losses limited the kingdom to the capital and its environs, which eventually collapsed altogether,
leaving it to others, including the Gutians, to fill the power vacuum
sporadically. Among Shar-kali-sharri's enemies were the Amorites at
Basar (perhaps modern Jebel el-Bishri, west of the middle Euphrates),
whom Sargon had also encountered there and about whom we will
hear much more.

The grandeur of this brief empire, especially that of Sargon and his
grandson Naram-Sin, became legendary, inspiring awe and envy for centuries. History has many examples of rulers who rose to power quickly and
fell just as rapidly, often commemorated by later generations in the creation of popular stories and legends. Such tales of culture heroes and
founders of great empires often obscure the realia that historians strive to
uncover (e.g., Cyrus, or Romulus and Remus).[41] Just so for Sargon of
Akkad, we have many such stories claiming to be copies of royal inscriptions that imitate older monumental inscriptions but that are actually from
a much later time.[42] The most striking example of this genre related to the
Old Akkadian period is the Legend of Sargon (also known as the Autobiography of Sargon).[43] The copies we have are from the first millennium
B.C.E., although it likely had a long history before the Neo-Assyrian period,
when it became popular.[44] Written in the first person, the account explains
that Sargon was an illegitimate son of a priestess who abandoned the baby
because her calling did not permit her to bear children. Its intent is to
explain Sargon's rapid and unexpected rise.

> I am Sargon the great king, king of Agade. ... My mother, the high priest-
> ess, conceived me, she bore me in secret. She placed me in a reed basket,
> she sealed my hatch with pitch. She left me to the river, whence I could
> not come up. The river carried me off, it brought me to Aqqi, drawer of
> water. Aqqi, drawer of water, brought me up as he dipped his bucket.
> Aqqi, drawer of water, raised me as his adopted son. Aqqi, drawer of
> water, set (me) to his orchard work. During my orchard work, Ishtar loved
> me. Fifty-five years I ruled as king. I became lord over and ruled the
> black-headed folk.[45]

The Legend of Sargon is of particular interest for readers of the Bible
because of its similarities to the narrative introducing Moses (Exod 2:1–10):
untimely pregnancy, concealed birth, abandonment of a newborn to river
waters, rescue, and adoption. This theme had forceful explanatory power
in the ancient world; the hero exposed at birth was rescued miraculously
and raised by another to become—unexpectedly—a ruler.

While later Babylonian traditions praised and admired Sargon, Naram-
Sin received a mixed assessment. The Sumerian composition Curse of
Akkad has survived in numerous copies, revealing its popularity in later

scribal schools. After describing Sargon's blessings owing to his support of the god Enlil at Nippur, the text describes Naram-Sin attacking Ekur, the temple of Enlil, destroying it completely. Enlil then sends the Gutian tribesmen from their mountainous homeland to punish Naram-Sin and bring the sacrilege of the Akkadian Dynasty to an end. Composed probably by Neo-Sumerian or Old Babylonian priests or scribes of Nippur, intending to warn all Babylonian rulers of the consequences of elevating any deity over Nippur's god Enlil, the Curse of Akkad is the first to portray Naram-Sin in the "misfortune-prone ruler" motif, which will be repeated in subsequent Babylonian literature, and illustrates the distinctly ambivalent perception of Naram-Sin among later Babylonians.[46]

The city of Akkad appears to have lost all political importance after the collapse of the Old Akkadian Dynasty, illustrated by the fact that we still have not identified its remains. Unimportant as it may have become politically, however, the enduring importance of this first Semitic empire—if indeed, it can legitimately be called an empire[47]—is indisputable. In addition to innovations in administration, language, economy, and religion, the Akkadian period produced masterful works of art, illustrated best by cylinder seals with detailed scenes of humans and animals impressive for their realism, and including new motifs from myths and legends not attested in the Early Dynastic periods. The vitality and realism of Old Akkadian art is also evident in sculpture, best illustrated by the so-called "Victory Stela" of Naram-Sin (see fig. 2.3), which has been called "one of the best works of ancient art," and in the famous life-size head of either Sargon or Naram-Sin, cast in bronze.[48]

Perhaps the most significant feature of the Akkadian legacy lies in the royal ideology of the Akkadian period. The new concept of monarchic sovereignty created by Sargon and carefully propagated by Naram-Sin inspired monarchs throughout the rest of Babylonian civilization. This first unification of Babylonia became the model for all subsequent royal aspirations. As we shall see, it was not an example easily followed or long sustained.

2.2.2. NEO-SUMERIAN PERIOD

The Sumerian King List describes a period of anarchy after Shar-kali-sharri's reign: "Who was king? Who was not king? Was Igigi king? Was Nanum king? Was Imi king? Was Elulu king? The four of them were kings and reigned three years."[49] The King List, in its schematic way, assigns the next period of Babylonian history to the Gutians, recording twenty or twenty-one Gutian kings who reigned a total of 125 years. But in point of fact, the spirit of independence among the old Sumerian city-states in the south reappeared and several of these regained local autonomy and prospered economically. The most notable of these was Lagash, where the

Fig. 2.3. Victory Stela of Naram-Sin.
King Naram-Sin of Akkad in horned tiara near a mountain summit, with
soldiers. Rose limestone stela (2230 B.C.E.). Originally from Mesopotamia—
found in Susa, Iran. 200 x 105 cm. Location: Louvre, Paris, France.
Photo Credit: Erich Lessing/Art Resource, NY.

ensi, Gudea (approximately 2141–2122 B.C.E.), rebuilt fifteen temples in Girsu, the administrative center of the Lagash state. This king is remarkable for the numerous statues and heads carved in stone discovered at Girsu, often depicting the ruler standing or sitting in reverential poses, and some of which bear inscriptions relating Gudea's great piety. These inscriptions also relate his raiding expeditions to the west for lumber to be used in his many building projects and once to Elam to acquire necessary spoils. When combined with two clay cylinders of poetic texts, these inscriptions represent Gudea's impressive literary legacy, which is the most extensive collection of classic Sumerian literature available to date.[50]

Thus southern Babylonia was experiencing a modest Sumerian "renaissance," while the north suffered from internal decline and the presence of foreign tribesmen, most notably the Gutians. Chronological precision is impossible because we presume an overlap between these developments in the south and the chaotic situation in the north. Despite the presentation of the King List, many of the Gutian "kings" in the north probably ruled only parts of the land and ruled those parts at the same time. Thus the amount of time between the Old Akkadian period and the next political entity of unified Babylonia is uncertain.[51]

In light of a resurgent Sumerian south and a weakened north, it is not surprising that liberation from the Gutians came from the south. A certain Utu-ḫegal, ruler of Uruk, finally drove the Gutians from Babylonia. After only seven years in power, however, Utu-ḫegal drowned, according to Babylonian tradition, and the mantel of power passed to his governor at Ur, whose name was Ur-Nammu.[52] It appears that Ur was at first eclipsed by Lagash as the leading city of the south. Eventually, however, Ur-Nammu is credited with founding the Third Dynasty of Ur (Ur III), so-called because the Sumerian King List marks two previous dynasties at the city of Ur in the Early Dynastic periods. The Third Dynasty of Ur, with its five kings (see fig. 2.4), established the next Babylonian empire, using harbors on the Euphrates to engage in trade to and from the Persian Gulf and the Indus Valley. An enormous number of cuneiform texts from this period illuminate a central bureaucracy, with holdings across a wide area of the

---

Fig. 2.4. Third Dynasty of Ur (Ur III), 2112–2004

Ur-Nammu, 2112–2095
Shulgi, 2094–2047
Amar-Sin, 2046–2038
Shu-Sin, 2037–2029
Ibbi-Sin, 2028–2004

ancient Near East indicating the extent of conquest. Sumerian once again became the official language of royal inscriptions, administration, and law.[53] The revitalization of Sumerian religion and culture generally reveals Ur III as a "Neo-Sumerian" period.

Ur-Nammu successfully ended the Gudea Dynasty at Lagash and expelled the Elamites from northern Babylonia. He eventually controlled the whole of Babylonia and assumed a new royal title emphasizing the unification of north and south: "King of Sumer [*Ki-engi*] and Akkad [*Ki-uri*]."[54] One of his year-date formulas is named simply for his making "straight the road from below to above," presumably referring to a trek across Babylonia from the Persian Gulf perhaps all the way to the Mediterranean. He may have been responsible for a collection of Neo-Sumerian laws, but his successor is possibly the one ultimately responsible (see below). Ur-Nammu's most sensational legacy is perhaps in the realm of architecture, since he was responsible for the building of various temples and shrines, including the famed ziggurat at Ur, now partially reconstructed.[55]

The appearance of a real Neo-Sumerian empire—again, if we should even use "empire"—occurred under Ur-Nammu's son and successor, Shulgi, who initiated administrative and economic reforms that transformed Ur into a centralized territorial state. His numerous military campaigns, detailed in his date formulas, illustrate his wide-reaching dominion along the northwest Euphrates and eastward in the Iranian plateau. In the twentieth to twenty-third years of his reign, Shulgi created an enormous bureaucratic apparatus and a standing army, redistributed land among military officials loyal to the crown, established schools for scribes, introduced innovations in bookkeeping and weights and measurements, and established a new calendar. Thousands of administrative and economic texts from the royal archives, easily the most numerous genre of cuneiform tablets now scattered in museums and private collections around the world, have illuminated an elaborate taxation system.[56] Many of these texts record the collection of sheep and other animals as well as all manner of perishable produce at revenue centers established in several cities in southern Babylonia. The administration of the empire was based on a distinction between the core and the periphery, the core being Babylonia proper and the periphery the provinces and cities in a military buffer zone to the east.[57]

At the head of this elaborate system stood King Shulgi himself, who governed the provinces and temple domains through a system of provincial governors and military generals, usually foreigners or family members loyal only to the crown. Such enormous social changes were accompanied by religious innovations. Shulgi's name, like Naram-Sin's before him, was written with the divine determinative (*dingir*). He became the object of worship at local temples in the land, apparently as a means of creating a royal ideology that would ensure control over independence-minded local rulers.

The reign of Shulgi may also be described as a period of great literary fluorescence. In addition to the ubiquitous administrative and economic texts, the new royal ideology of divine kingship yielded an impressive corpus of royal hymns.[58] In addition, Shulgi is possibly responsible for creating legal institutions that resulted in the first official code of laws in human history.[59]

The Neo-Sumerian law code consists of casuistic laws framed by a prologue and an epilogue (now missing).[60] This literary structure served as the model for subsequent codes of law in the ancient world, as we shall see, including Lipit-Ishtar of Isin, Hammurapi of Babylon, and the Israelite collection in Exod 21–23. In light of this literary productivity, it is not surprising that even the Sumerian King List has now been attributed to Shulgi.[61]

Shulgi was followed by two of his sons, Amar-Sin and Shu-Sin, both of whom also claimed divinity but about which we know little else.[62] Amar-Sin enjoyed the military prowess characteristic of his father and devoted himself to architectural enterprises, particularly in Nippur and the capital city, Ur. Later traditions contain the tantalizing detail that he died from "the bite" of a shoe, which has variously been taken to mean a gangrenous foot.[63] Shu-Sin encountered and suppressed resistance in the eastern provinces, but the more serious threat to his empire emerged early in his reign from the west. Just as Old Akkadian rulers before him had encountered the western Semitic Amorites, so now Shu-Sin's hold on the Ur III Empire was jeopardized by their presence. His fourth year-date formula was "year (when) the wall of Amurru was built," and other traditions named the wall "keeping away Tidnum," one of the Amorite tribes.[64] As a sort of ancient Maginot Line, this Amorite Wall was intended to stem the tide of immigrants into Babylonia's heartland from Syria, where drought had likely forced the Amorite tribes to seek pasturage in the irrigated river lands. While Shu-Sin met modest success in these efforts, his successor, Ibbi-Sin, was forced to build further walls and fortifications closer to home. Slowly the provinces withdrew their loyalty and the empire was lost during Ibbi-Sin's reign. The city of Ur was so ravaged by enemies from the eastern frontiers that the destruction left an indelible mark on the Babylonian psyche. The trauma of the event contributed to an important literary motif in subsequent Sumero-Akkadian literature, the "city-lament," which survived for centuries and which shares numerous features with the biblical book of Lamentations and several psalms.[65]

2.3. THE CITY OF BABYLON

The city of Babylon itself has been conspicuously absent in our story thus far. Potsherds have been reported from the surface of the site from the latter part of the Early Dynastic period, so we know the city existed as early as the mid-third millennium B.C.E.[66] Excavations of the city have been largely limited to the Neo-Babylonian levels because of the rise of ground water, and it has not been possible to do much with deeper and earlier strata. Therefore, archaeology is of little help in tracing Babylon's role in these early periods or in determining if it had political significance at all.

For the earliest history of Babylon, we are limited to the literary references from antiquity, which preserve several interesting but contradictory traditions on the founding and naming of the city. The first reference to the city of Babylon comes from chronographic and omen literature, which attribute the name of the city to Sargon of Akkad. He allegedly dug up a mound of dust from Babylon and set it up near his own city of Akkad in a symbolic act stressing his role as conqueror. It was at this time that he named the place "Babylon."[67] Sargon's great grandson, Shar-kali-sharri, commemorated the construction of two new temples in Babylon.[68] During the Neo-Sumerian period, Babylon was a relatively unimportant provincial capital with a local governor (ensi).

Once the city of Babylon rose to political preeminence under Hammurapi (see ch. 3), its naming is no longer a royal achievement but is elevated to a divine pronouncement. In the opening paragraphs of the Code of Hammurapi, the naming of the city is attributed to the gods Anu and Enlil, who "named the city of Babylon with its august name and made it supreme within the regions of the world." They also gave supreme power to the Babylonian deity, Marduk, for whom they established eternal kingship within the city. Simultaneously, according to the prologue, Anu and Enlil gave Hammurapi his name, so that he might provide pious justice and peace to the region.[69] Thus the prologue creates an ideological nexus of city, deity, and king, which demonstrates the importance of Babylon during what has come to be known as the Old Babylonian period. Similarly, in the Babylonian Creation Epic (the so-called *Enūma Eliš*), Marduk himself announces that he has built and named the city as residence for his divine fathers: "I shall call [its] name [Babylon], (meaning) "Houses of the Great Gods.""[70]

Before leaving the ancient literary references related to the naming of Babylon, we must of course consider the ancient Hebrew account of the naming of Babylon in the derogatory interpretation given for the name in Gen 11:9. Whereas Akkadian speakers had used popular etymology to contrive an exalted meaning "Gate of God" (see ch. 1), Genesis uses a

Hebrew wordplay to refute the lofty claim: "Therefore it was called Babel [*bābel*], because there the Lord confused [*bālal*] the language of all the earth" (Gen 11:9). In this view, the city of Babylon represents humanity's unified rebellion against God and was therefore marked by confusion (*bālal*), thereby turning the "gate of heaven" into "confusion of speech" and the dispersion of humanity.[71] More generally, the tower of Babel pericope illustrates early Israel's suspicion and distrust of urbanization. For the ancient Babylonian, city life was the divinely prescribed form of human civilization, but for Israel the confusion of tongues and monumental architecture symbolized all that was wrong with prideful Babylonian culture. The conflict of worldviews was undeniable.

3

THE OLD BABYLONIAN PERIOD—A NEW WORLD POWER

Toward the end of the third millennium B.C.E., the Sumero-Akkadian culture of southern Mesopotamia had advanced remarkably with regard to literature, economics, religion, the arts, and so forth. Most of these advances occurred gradually and simultaneously with certain sociopolitical forces, culminating in the first experiments at empire building in human civilization. As the second millennium B.C.E. dawned, significant sociopolitical and cultural developments were taking place that would impact the future of Babylonia for centuries. During the first half of the millennium, the city of Babylon rose from relative obscurity to become the political center of the country and then an empire of such magnitude and renown that it would leave an indelible mark on the rest of human history. The rise of Babylon took place in the eighteenth century B.C.E., yet its legacy is such that we follow scholarly convention by calling the entire era the Old Babylonian Period (2003–1595 B.C.E.).

3.1. ARRIVAL OF THE AMORITES IN MESOPOTAMIA

The Bible speaks of "Amorites" as tribes who occupied portions of Canaan prior to Israel's arrival ("Amorite" being the anglicized form of Hebrew *ʾĕmōrî*). With the retrieval and decipherment of ancient Babylonian texts over the past 150 years, it was discovered that the term "Amorite" had a long history. We first read of Amorites in texts of the third millennium, in which the Sumerians called them m a r . t u, while Akkadian speakers used *amurru* and *amurrû*.[1] In both Sumerian and Akkadian, the term may be either directional ("west") or ethnogeographical (*AHw* 1:46; *CAD* A/2:92–95). Although it is impossible to determine which meaning might have been primary, the evidence from Ebla reveals the existence of a geographical region bearing the name Martu, located west of Sumer but not west of Ebla. Sumerian appears therefore to have derived the directional meaning from this geographical designation, and it came secondarily to denote a people living in the northwest.[2]

The role of the Amorites in ancient Near Eastern history can only be reconstructed in part, due to a severe lack of firsthand information.[3] The only evidence we have for the Amorite language is found in personal names, which however is enough to identify it as closely related to the West Semitic family of languages to which Biblical Hebrew belongs. In these names, Amorite speakers are distinguished by certain spellings (e.g., initial *y* where we would expect *w*), by vocabulary words (e.g., *ʿabdu* for "slave" rather than the standard Akkadian *wardum,* and *malku* for "king" rather than *šarrum*), and by the use of West Semitic deities in the names.[4] The Amorites were so thoroughly assimilated into the Sumero-Akkadian culture, it is unlikely that their own language was ever written, and we are therefore deprived of their native sources.

Migrations from Syria (especially the Ḫabur and Baliḫ river valleys in the northwest bend of the Euphrates) into the alluvial plain of southern Mesopotamia were nearly constant in ancient history, and this was not necessarily perceived as unusual or alarming for those living in the wealthier city-states of Babylonia. This was especially so if the migrations were gradual and peaceful. It used to be popular among historians of the ancient Near East to speak of "waves of Semites from the desert" flowing into Mesopotamia, thus implying a *Völkerwanderungstheorie* (a now-outmoded "mass-migrations theory") that postulated the physical removal of nomadic pastoralists in mass migrations. Specifically, Mesopotamian history would be portrayed as having been shaped largely by four Semitic migrations: Akkadian, Amorite, Aramean, and Arab.[5] In a simplistic way, historical transitions could be explained as the result of established cultures losing control of their urban centers to invading and disruptive nomadic groups, which were often blamed for breaks in occupation levels or even destruction levels. In more recent approaches, cultural anthropologists have offered a corrective, emphasizing the often-symbiotic relationships between nomads and urban dwellers in antiquity and explaining that historical transitions result from the convergence of numerous factors, including economic, climatic, and social causes.[6]

On the other hand, this new balanced approach must take into consideration the evidence that the Amorites were, in fact, efficient militarily, which is demonstrated by at least two facts. First, Neo-Sumerian kings had hired their military expertise for protection of some of the cities, but once the empire collapsed, cities throughout Babylonia were so quickly dominated by Amorite dynasties that it appears they simply took over the cities they once protected. They appear to have simply moved from tent dwellings outside the city walls to the palace inside the city. Second, Old Babylonian military titles are characterized by Amorite designations, indicating their expertise in the area. For example, "headman of the Amorites" and "chief of the Amorites" were types of generals, and "scribe of the Amorites" was a quartermaster.[7] However, in spite of occasional conflict between the last of the Neo-Sumerian kings and Amorite groups, and in spite of the explanations given in Sumerian sources, blame for the fall of Ur and the loss of the empire must rest with a combination of sociopolitical features, including imperialistic over-extension, social unrest and internal decay, independence-minded city centers in some of the provinces, in addition to the pressures created by the growing incursions of Amorites and other groups.[8]

As we have seen, the Amorites begin to appear in numbers during the Old Akkadian Dynasty, some dating to Shar-kali-sharri, and others probably dating back to Naram-Sin.[9] The early Amorites were pastoral nomads, related to each other no doubt in tribes. The m a r t u of the Neo-Sumerian period may refer only to the most important tribe, but it more likely denotes a confederation of several tribes. The Sumerian myth Marriage of Martu may describe the general perception of the individual Amorite: "He is a tent-dweller, [buffeted by] wind and rain, [who knows not] offerings, he digs up *truffles* in the highlands, knows not how to bend the knee, eats uncooked meat, has no house in his lifetime, is not brought to burial when he dies."[10] The picture of a wholly uncivilized individual who lives in an unsheltered tent, eats raw meat, and fails to worship or bury the dead properly is no doubt an exaggeration, but one that illustrates the conflict between urbanized Sumerians and the early Amorites. The kings of Ur sometimes raided Amorite tribes; at other times used them as military mercenaries or territorial officers. Eventually the increasing number of Amorites led Shu-Sin to build a defensive "Amorite Wall" in a vain attempt to keep them out of the heartland of Sumer. The Amorites must have disrupted Ur's administrative hold on the provinces so that various city centers could assert their independence. So the Amorites were a definite contributing factor to the fall of the Neo-Sumerian Empire, but they were certainly not the sole cause, as has often been overstated.

The four centuries following the Neo-Sumerian Empire may be characterized as the age of the Amorites. Repeated everywhere across the Tigris-Euphrates valley was a process of gradual sedentarization and acculturation in which Amorites eventually became the dominant population of Mesopotamia's leading cities. At least this is the evidence of the overwhelmingly widespread use of Amorite personal names. By 1900 B.C.E. individuals are no longer designated as "Amorite" (mar.tu), presumably because it was no longer unusual or unique to encounter them. The newcomers established new political centers at cities across the ancient Near East, the most important of which were Isin, Larsa, Eshnunna, and Kish in southern Mesopotamia, Mari and Ashur further north, and Qatna and Aleppo in the northwest. At the previously insignificant city of Babylon, on the banks of the Araḫtum canal of the Euphrates, an Amorite named Sumu-abum established a dynasty in 1894 B.C.E. that would eventually carry the city to new heights of political and cultural significance.

Although the Old Babylonian period in general offers a wealth of diverse documentation and resources, our knowledge of Amorite culture and society in particular is sadly limited without the benefit of Amorite texts. In order to learn much at all about the society and culture of these Amorite groups, we must go beyond the boundaries of Babylonia proper to the city of Mari on the west bank of the Euphrates at modern Tell Hariri.[11] If it were not for the extensive archives from the kingdom period of Mari's history, we would know practically nothing of Amorite tribal structure. Thanks to the nearly 25,000 documents discovered at Mari, the last half of the eighteenth and first half of the seventeenth centuries B.C.E. are better known than most and shed remarkable light on Amorite tribal life. This archive has illuminated a number of Amorite tribal confederations, the two most dominant of which were the DUMU.MEŠ *sim'al* (i.e., Binu Sim'al or Sim'alites, literally "sons of the left") and DUMU.MEŠ *yamina* (i.e., Binu Yamina or Yaminites, literally "sons of the right").[12] In fact, the Mari archives have also revealed how Zimri-Lim, powerful king of Mari during the early eighteenth century B.C.E., functioned as an Amorite (specifically a "Sim'alite") tribal state, balancing his roles as Amorite tribesman and king of an urban-based empire.[13] Although this may be quite different from the Amorite city-states of southern Mesopotamia, it raises interesting questions about our traditional assumptions that tribal groups necessarily abandoned their patrimonial structures when establishing new urban-based state authorities and about assumed conflict between "town and tribe." Furthermore, the Amorite Dynasty of the city of Babylon, which came eventually to dominate this period of history, apparently maintained a link with the Yaminite tribes of Amnanû and Yaḥrirû.[14]

3.2. The Isin-Larsa Period and the Rise of Babylon

Despite the absence of political unity during the first two centuries of this period (2000–1800 B.C.E.), the emergence of the Amorites resulted in an amazing cultural cohesion. Their apparent control of nearly every regional capital and their swelling ranks in the general population (given the evidence of personal names) resulted in "a new cultural koine," which blended Amorite traditions with the older Sumero-Akkadian culture.[15] Sumerian features of the new cultural milieu were especially venerated in southern Mesopotamia, although the Sumerian language was no longer widely spoken there and survived primarily as an official and literary language.[16] Akkadian eventually became the new international language, used as far away as Syria-Palestine, Anatolia, and the plains of Iran. The spread of a new Semitic *lingua franca* may be explained not only by the influence of the powerful eighteenth-century empire at Babylon but by the existence of this new Amorite cultural koine.

The new Amorite culture emerged at numerous cities in Babylonia after the collapse of the Neo-Sumerian Empire. In the fragmentation that ensued, two rival powers emerged: the dynasties at the cities of Isin and Larsa (see fig. 3.1).[17] Both claimed to be legitimate successors to Ur's imperial might and, in Isin's case, assumed the traditional title "King of Sumer and Akkad." Interestingly, the Sumerian King List concludes with the dynasty of Isin, which illustrates the royal ambition of Isin's kings to locate themselves in the old Sumerian tradition of right of kingship.[18] In reality, the parallel dynasties of Isin and Larsa had to be content with sharing the region and the imperial resources, neither being powerful enough to dominate the other for protracted periods of time. There were temporary victories of one city over the other, but the fact that they coexisted for two centuries less than one hundred miles apart illustrates their inability to exert the kind of strength required for imperial dominance.

During this Isin-Larsa period of Babylonian history, the city of Nippur emerged as a great scribal center, where old Sumerian "classics" were preserved and new compositions created, most in praise of the kings of Isin or Larsa. This literary legacy also preserved a collection of laws promulgated by Lipit-Ishtar, fifth king of the Isin Dynasty.[19] Composed in Sumerian, the laws follow the now-traditional format of Ur-Nammu (see ch. 2), by framing casuistic laws with a prologue and epilogue. The collection has

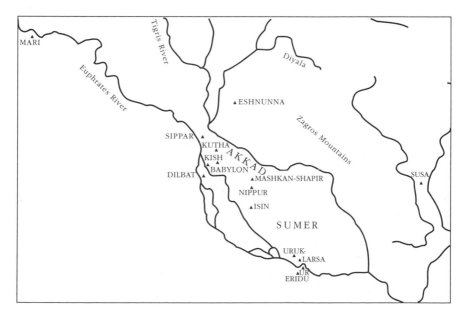

Fig. 3.1. Old Babylonian Period.

survived in over fifteen copies, mostly from Nippur, which preserve the prologue, epilogue, and almost fifty laws, although many of the laws themselves are poorly preserved.

By around 1800 B.C.E. the Amorite culture was firmly ensconced in cities throughout southern Mesopotamia and had come to power in the form of new royal dynasties in several of those cities. Political events in Babylonia over the next fifteen hundred years may be grouped into "middle," "new," and "late" stages, meaning this era covering approximately the first half of the second millennium is rightly known as the Old Babylonian period. Archaeological evidence from Babylon itself is of almost no help in reconstructing events, because despite the significant material remains from the Neo-Babylonian period, the very high water table means the site has produced almost nothing from preceding periods. Fortunately, many important events during the Old Babylonian period may be reconstructed because of the scribal practice of naming each year of a king's reign after a major royal activity occurring in the previous year, usually cultic or military. Such "year-name" labels (also known as "year-dates" or "year-formulas") were then used to date legal or administrative documents. The practice began in the Old Akkadian period (e.g., "the year Sargon went [on a campaign] to Simurrum")[20] and continued throughout the Old Babylonian period.[21] These year-names will be an important resource in the reconstruction that follows.

3.3. Hammurapi's Empire

The first five rulers of the new Amorite Dynasty at Babylon, sometimes called the "First Dynasty of Babylon," did little to distinguish themselves, especially in ways that would foresee Babylon's potential (see fig. 3.2). They were occupied primarily with building activities, mostly local fortifications and temples, mentioned frequently in their year-names. So, for example, Sumu-la-el boasts mainly of digging canals, building Babylon's defense walls, and establishing "a throne-dais, completed with gold and silver" for Marduk's exalted sanctuary, although there are a few references to plundering Kish and its walls. Likewise, Sabium (re)built Esagil of Marduk in Babylon, as well as Ebabbar of Shamash in Sippar, and repaired other temples and walls in central Babylonia.[22] These repaired temples and other building projects in surrounding cities by the first five rulers of the dynasty suggest that Babylon had already grown into a significant power in the region, due to the resources required to build them and support the priestly staff of each.[23]

These first rulers also conducted military campaigns and apparently exercised a degree of authority in certain neighboring cities (such as

Fig. 3.2. Old Babylonian Kings of Babylon, Larsa, and Mari

Larsa	Babylon	Mari
Sumu-el (1894–1866)	Sumu-abum (1894–1881)	
	Sumu-la-el (1880–1845)	
Nur-Adad (1865–1850)		
Sin-iddinam (1849–1843)	Sabium (1844–1831)	
Sin-eribam (1842–1841)		
Sin-iqisham (1840–1836)		
Ṣilli-Adad (1835)		
Warad-Sin (1834–1823)	Apil-Sin (1830–1813)	
		Yaggid-Lim (1820–1811)
Rim-Sin (1822–1763)		
	Sin-muballit (1812–1793)	Yaḫdun-Lim (1810–1795)
	Hammurapi (1792–1750)	Sumu-Yamam (1794–1791)
		Yasmaḫ-Addu (1790–1776)
		Zimri-Lim (1775–1760)
	Samsu-iluna (1749–1712)	
	Abi-eshuḫ (1711–1684)	
	Ammi-ditana (1683–1647)	
	Ammi-ṣaduqa (1646–1626)	
	Samsu-ditana (1625–1595)	

Sippar and Kish), but no real territorial control can be accredited to them. During the reign of the fifth dynast, Sin-muballit (1812–1793), a number of political powers in and around Mesopotamia began vying for supremacy. These were predominantly Eshnunna to the east, the ever-dangerous Elamites further east, and Shamshi-Adad in the north at what would become an Old Assyrian Empire. In Babylonia proper, the old rival dynasties of Isin and Larsa were still a threat, although Isin was now in decline. At Larsa, a ruler named Rim-Sin came to the throne at an early age, judging by his sixty-year reign.[24] In Rim-Sin's fourteenth year, he established a degree of supremacy over at least the south with a victory against a coalition led by Uruk and including Sin-muballit of Babylon.[25] Rim-Sin was the new force of southern Mesopotamia to watch, although Sin-muballit continued on the throne of Babylon, where he continued to build fortifications.

In this delicate balance of power, Sin-muballit left his throne to his son, Hammurapi (1792–1750).[26] A word may be in order here on the spelling of the name, since I have used *p* instead of the traditional *b* in "Hammurabi." The cuneiform spelling of the name can be read either way, and because the sign used for the last syllable in most occurrences of the name is primarily *bi* and only secondarily *pi,* it was originally (and logically) assumed his name should be spelled Hammurabi. The name most likely has two components: *ḫammu-* and *-rap/bi,* both of which present problems of interpretation. Assuming a West Semitic (Amorite) origin for the name, we may assume that the first element is "paternal uncle" or "kinsman," meaning "Divine Kinsman" (although this is far from certain), while the second element is "he/it heals" if read with *p,* but "mighty" if read with *b.* As if this were not enough to sort out, the clarity brought about by the alphabetic cuneiform of Ugarit, which at first appears to settle the question entirely, does not put the issue to rest sat-isfactorily. A number of Ugaritic kings from the second millennium bore the name ʿ*mrp,* which appears to be parallel etymologically, and so con-firms "Ḫammu-rapi" as "The Divine Kinsman Heals." But we have additional evidence from the west (Alalaḫ) that calls this understanding into question.[27] I have adopted the spelling with *p* but admit that the problem appears intractable at the moment.

Earlier scholarship tended to portray the "age of Hammurapi" as a Babylonia-centered phenomenon, which is not surprising considering the extent of the empire built by Hammurapi and its subsequent legacy. But a large number of contemporary documents from this period (particularly the archives from Mari) have corrected this notion and portray rather a cos-mopolitan Near East with a multicentered base of political power shared by several cities. A now-famous letter from Mari—one invariably quoted in this context and not to be missed here—contains the following political assessment of international affairs as observed by a certain Itûr-Asdu, an official of King Zimri-Lim of Mari: "There is no king who, of himself, is the strongest. Ten or fifteen kings follow Hammurapi of Babylon, the same number follow Rim-Sin of Larsa, the same number follow Ibal-pi-El of Eshnunna, the same number follow Amut-pi-il of Qatanum [Qatna], twenty kings follow Yarim-Lim of Yamhad [Aleppo]."[28] The precise date of this assessment is not given in the letter, but it probably comes from around the middle of Hammurapi's reign and reflects his standing among the other leading powers of his day. Thus a balance of power resulted because no single state could boast superiority in natural and human resources, so the more ambitious rulers strengthened their hand with coalitions and diplomacy.

This balance of power allowed Hammurapi to devote his energies in the first years of his reign to defensive and religious building activities and internal administration. Of his first twenty-nine years, only a few of his year-date formulas record military campaigns. Specifically, we should note his seventh, tenth, and eleventh years (1786, 1783, and 1782 B.C.E., respectively), in which Hammurapi took control of several cities, the most important of which were Uruk and Isin.[29] However, it should be cautioned that Hammurapi was conducting these military forays not as an independent ruler but as a member of a coalition with sometimes more powerful rulers.[30] In his second date-formula, he is said to have "established justice [*mīšarum*] in the country," an apparent reference to legal reforms that may have culminated in his famous law code (see below).[31]

Although Hammurapi's predecessors appear to have left him in a position of strength, our best reconstruction of political events during these early years of his reign suggest a humble beginning overall. His neighbor to the north, Shamshi-Adad, commanded the favorable position, occupying Mari and controlling the middle Euphrates valley. It was only through an adroit use of shifting coalitions that Hammurapi was able to avoid being overrun by Shamshi-Adad or by the dangerous armies of Eshnunna to his north and Larsa to his south. The politics of the age demanded such tenuous alliances, so that a "king's success was a function of the king's skill in maneuvering the counters of this dangerous game."[32] Hammurapi seems to have fragmented his opposition cleverly during this time with diplomatic activity, all while he was carefully building his own power base.[33] The stellar rise of Babylon is perhaps a tribute to Hammurapi as a man of personal genius and exceptional gifts, a leader who left an indelible mark on his successors.

Once Shamshi-Adad died (ca. 1782 B.C.E.) Assyrian strength waned, and Mari was able to regain independence under Zimri-Lim. Over the next decade or so Hammurapi fortified strategic cities in northern Babylonia, while accepting an uneasy coalition with Rim-Sin of Larsa. It was a relationship of convenience for mutual defense, necessary only because of the geographical proximity of Babylon and Larsa. While Hammurapi maintained the truce, Rim-Sin subdued Isin, Uruk, and other potentially

**Fig. 3.3. Head of an Old Babylonian ruler,
commonly assumed to be Hammurapi.**
From Susa. Diorite, height: 15 cm. Location: Louvre, Paris, France.
Photo Credit: Erich Lessing/Art Resource, NY.

hostile cities to Babylon's south. Then, when Hammurapi felt secure in his position, he embarked on aggressive military campaigns aimed at consolidating his personal hold on southern Mesopotamia (carefully preserved in his year-date formulas). In his thirtieth year (1763 B.C.E.), a year that marks a distinct turning point in his reign, Hammurapi successfully defeated an Elamite coalition army comprised of troops from Assyria, Eshnunna, and elsewhere. His thirty-first year saw victory at last over his neighbor at Larsa, Rim-Sin. After these victories, Hammurapi for the first time began to use the brazen titulary from the great third-millennium empires in his year-date formulas. His thirtieth year was one in which he "consolidated the foundations of the empire of Sumer and Akkad," and in his thirty-first year Hammurapi claims to have forced Sumer and Akkad to obey his orders.[34]

With the fall of Larsa, all the rival cities of the south had fallen to Hammurapi's possession. For the first time since the Neo-Sumerian Empire at Ur, all of southern Mesopotamia was united under a single throne. Meanwhile, Hammurapi enjoyed a mutually beneficial relationship with Zimri-Lim of Mari, since letters between the two reveal cooperation on numerous common goals. The two kings allowed ambassadors to report on military and political situations observed in the respective cities, even to the degree of requesting and exchanging contingents of troops. However, the relationship had long been one of "trust but verify," since each had good reason to be suspicious of the other.[35] Now that Hammurapi controlled the south, this friendly cooperation was destined to end, and in his thirty-third year (1760) Hammurapi took possession of Mari, although it does not appear likely this involved military conquest.[36] Regardless of the specifics of how Mari fell, it is clear that over the next two years Hammurapi plundered its treasures before completely destroying the walls of Mari in 1758. In his thirty-seventh, thirty-eighth, and thirty-ninth years he subdued Eshnunna and other lesser threats in Assyria to the north. For the last portion of his reign, the whole of Mesopotamia proper was his. Only the western kingdoms of Aleppo and Qatna were beyond his reach.

The prologue to Hammurapi's law code (see below) proudly lists the prominent cities of Mesopotamia that were subject to him, including the older influential cities of the south, the Assyrian centers in the north, and those along the Middle Euphrates.[37] His royal titles use expressions from the powerful Old Akkadian Empire in a new way, and Hammurapi clearly viewed himself a successor to the first great empires of the third millennium. In his thirty-third year, he "reorganized Sumer and Akkad from confusion."[38] Although the empire built by Hammurapi may have rivaled that of the Neo-Sumerian period in geographical extent, the same cannot be said of its duration, as we shall see.

3.4. Hammurapi's Dynasty

The sons and successors of Hammurapi number five, and they retained control of the empire for the next century and a half after his death (see chart on p. 41 for names and dates). This duration marks the relative success of the dynasty, though in certain respects Babylonia could hardly be termed an "empire" during many of these years. Merely a decade after Hammurapi's death, in the ninth year-name of his son, Samsu-iluna, we have a record of the first encounter with a new element in Babylonian history, the Kassites.[39] They appear again in the third year of Samsu-iluna's son, Abi-eshuḫ (1711–1684). Their appearance is not particularly revealing, but their continued presence is an indication of the inability of Babylon to maintain the imperialistic dominance it once enjoyed. In general, only twenty years after the death of Hammurapi, the rise of the new kingdom of Hana along the Euphrates in the northwest (with Terqa as a capital) resulted in the loss of the territory taken from Mari.[40]

Samsu-iluna reigned thirty-seven years, which may attest to his creative longevity more than to the genuine strength of his kingdom.[41] Upon succeeding his father, Samsu-iluna immediately established "freedom (from taxation) for Sumer and Akkad," according to his second year-name. Such restoration edicts (*mīšarum, AHw* 659–60; *CAD* M/2, 116–19; or *andurārum, AHw* 50–51; *CAD* A/2, 115–17) were intended by royal decree to counteract the burden of indebtedness, in order to remedy economic malfunctions by the remission of debts, both for state agents and non-commercial debts of private individuals.[42] The best example we have is from the Edict of Ammi-ṣaduqa (1646–1626), the next-to-last king in the dynasty, which he issued at the beginning of his reign and which illustrates in great detail how the edict worked, including how certain business investments counted as exceptions.[43] Interestingly, Ammi-ṣaduqa's edict contains a reference distinguishing Amorites from Akkadians, indicating that in the middle of the seventeenth century B.C.E. the Amorites continued to be a distinct ethnic identity.[44] From this time forward, they were completely merged into the population and disappear from native cuneiform records.

Such royal edicts were not new, since Hammurapi had boasted of such action in his second and twenty-second years and had made *mīšarum* (in this case better translated "justice") an important raison d'être for his reign, as commissioned by Shamash, and made clear in the prologue to his law code. Nor was the practice an innovation in Hammurapi's day. We know of such cases in Isin and Larsa, and it can be traced back to the "reforms" of Uru-inimgina (ch. 2), making it clear that Babylonian society in general valued economic equality and fairness and shunned exploitation. But Hammurapi was genuinely obsessed either with economic justice or with portraying himself as the justice-giver, and his prestige resulted in the issuing of such *mīšarum* decrees at the beginning of nearly every Old Babylonian king to follow him.[45]

Although Samsu-iluna's *mīšarum* decree in his second year-name may be intended as a boast of his ability to provide such economic relief, the frequency of such decrees during the rest of the dynasty increased, and this reflects a weakened economy generally. One of the striking changes of Old Babylonian times, and indeed of the new Amorite culture generally, was the amount of private enterprise recorded in letters and contracts, which are abundant, especially in and around Babylon itself. During the reigns of Hammurapi's successors, administrative bureaucracy swelled, reflected in a growing number of offices and titles, even while social and economic deterioration became more acute. Coupled with the pressure of a growing number of foreign influences, especially in the north, this internal decay eventually resulted in a rather meager domain for Hammurapi's successors, who ruled an empire nothing like that shaped by Hammurapi himself. The amount of territory under Babylon's control had been greatly reduced, due to a combination of this economic pressure and the arrival of the Kassites in the north, in addition to a dynasty in the south that later tradition would call the "First Sealand Dynasty."

However, the final blow came from elsewhere. In 1595, it was Indo-Europeans from Anatolia, the Hittites, who administered the final blow to Babylon.[46] Under Murshili I (1620–1595 B.C.E.), they swept through the Euphrates corridor, attacking and capturing Babylon. The Hittites, however, withdrew immediately, taking away Babylon's treasures and leaving behind them a power vacuum. This vacuum was filled readily and willingly by the Kassites, and the next phase of Babylonian history was under way. The brief but impressive unification of Mesopotamia under the First Dynasty of Babylon left a mark on the collective psyche of the country and created a new role for the previously insignificant city. Because of the grandeur and strength of this brief empire, all of southern Mesopotamia would henceforth be "Babylonia." No city would rival Babylon for the next two millennia, until the Greeks built Seleucia.[47]

3.5. OLD BABYLONIAN LITERATURE, CULTURE, AND LEGACY

As we have seen, Babylonia first rose to a prestigious role in world history during Hammurapi's reign. Fortunately, we have a variety of historical, legal, and epistolary texts from the Old Babylonian period. Additionally numerous works, which we may be justified in calling the Babylonian belles-lettres, were preserved by repeated copying in scribal schools. In fact, although there are other periods of history in southern Mesopotamia with larger numbers of texts (i.e., administrative texts from Neo-Sumerian and Neo-Babylonian periods), the Old Babylonian period has yielded the largest numbers across all text types used in the culture.[48] In other words, we have a greater variety in the documentation and therefore a more complete picture of the Old Babylonian period than any other.

The amalgamation of the third-millennium Sumero-Akkadian culture with the Amorite culture in the Old Babylonian period is reflected in interesting developments in the primary languages of the day, Sumerian and Akkadian. As we have seen, Sumerian was dead or dying as a spoken language but was retained as a high-literary language. Its cuneiform script was retained as well, although its ideographic pictograms were modified substantially for the needs of inflected Akkadian.[49] In the Old Babylonian period, Sumerian was typically used for legal documents and Sumerian literary texts of the now-venerated older culture, while Akkadian was used for letters and certain Akkadian literature.

The Babylonians were clearly infatuated with the Sumero-Akkadian culture of the third millennium, so much so that they adapted and propagated that culture to a large extent. The Sumerians had been true cultural innovators, not only in the invention of writing but in establishing literary forms. The Amorites of the Old Babylonian period preserved what was by then a declining culture, and many of the Babylonian masterpieces are adaptations of the older Sumerian versions. Although most of our documentation from the Old Akkadian and Neo-Sumerian periods is administrative, we have enough fragments of literary texts to illustrate that a literary tradition was continuous in the late third millennium B.C.E.[50] But it is not until the Old Babylonian period that we may be justified in speaking of a literary fluorescence, in which the rise of an extensive written literature occurred for the first time in human history. Rather than a sudden burst of Babylonian genius, this period was one of copying and preserving Sumerian traditions now venerated as quite ancient, and to a lesser degree composing new literature, especially royal hymns, scientific literature, and mathematical and geometrical texts.[51]

Much of what we know of Sumerian and early Babylonian literature was preserved at Nippur and Ur in houses of learning, or scribal "schools" (Sumerian é.dub.ba.a; Akkadian *bīt ṭuppi,* literally, "tablet house").[52] These schools had been established by Shulgi toward the end of the third millennium but flourished in the Old Babylonian period as never before. Such schools began as temple annexes, but by the first half of the second millennium they were attached to palaces and eventually some were privatized. Most of our information about the schools and about education generally comes from numerous student/teacher exercises, lexical lists, essays on school life, examination texts, and royal hymns in which certain kings make reference to their school days. These texts often describe fascinating pedagogical methods employed by various administrators, including a principal (the "father of the Edubba") and his assistants (advanced students, or "big brothers"), who checked tablets produced and copied by students and heard memorized lessons.[53] The teacher would write an exercise on the obverse of a tablet, and the student would copy the lesson on the reverse (see fig. 3.4). Most of these "school tablets" are round in shape, and we have many examples of them in various stages of quality. Scribal students were provided with a comprehensive curriculum, which is similar enough at Nippur and Ur to suggest it was standardized and which appears to have been based on two or three subjects: cuneiform writing, Sumerian language (which was now "foreign" enough to require formal study), and mathematics. Although we have no way of estimating how widespread such education was generally, it seems likely that literacy reached a peak in the Old Babylonian period and that "writing permeated society more thoroughly than at any time until the introduction of the alphabet."[54]

In view of the unprecedented political significance of the Babylonians during the Old Babylonian period and their continued veneration for generations, they contributed significantly to the common Semitic cultural heritage throughout ancient Near Eastern history. Therefore certain literary contributions (as best as we can determine their dates of composition) and cultural features merit discussion here. The Babylonians themselves did not divide literature into specific categories. In general, however, we may speak of "epics" (dealing with the memorable deeds of humans), "myths" (devoted to the exploits of gods),[55] as well as prayers and hymns, essays, wisdom literature, and historiography.

Arguably the greatest literary piece to come from Babylonian soil is the Gilgamesh Epic. Because the ancients often titled literary compositions according to the first few words of the text, this piece is also entitled He Who Saw Everything. Most critical editions are based on the twelve-tablet standard version known to us from the much-later library at Ashurbanipal's Nineveh, which included more than one copy of the work. The recensional history of the Gilgamesh Epic is complex, and much remains to be determined.[56] So, for example, even the copies of the Gilgamesh Epic found at Neo-Assyrian Nineveh have different arrangements of tablets and columns. The widest geographical spread of copies of the Epic occurred during the Kassite period (see ch. 4 below). Old Babylonian copies of the Epic have been discovered at different locations in southern Mesopotamia, and it appears—although this is far from certain—that this is when the previously disparate Sumerian stories about the great third-millennium king were first woven together into a continuous, integrated epic.[57] Yet the so-called "Old Babylonian Version" of the Epic is no mere translation of Sumerian precursors; rather, it is an epic of nearly one thousand lines of fresh and vibrant poetry. The Epic tells the touching account of how the ancient king

Fig. 3.4. An Old Babylonian school tablet using a Sumerian proverb as an exercise. The instructor's assignment is on the obverse (top) and the student's copy on the reverse (bottom). © Copyright The British Museum.

of Uruk (see ch. 2 for discussion of his historicity) rebelled against death when he lost his friend Enkidu.[58] Through too many twists and turns to summarize here, the Epic follows the hero through numerous adventures and travels, meeting and conquering distant regions and monsters, but in the end he is forced to recognize his own mortality. Finally, Gilgamesh returns to Uruk and accepts the splendor of the great city as his enduring accomplishment, and with it the realization that the human individual is destined to work, to build, to enjoy, and then to die. The theme of the Epic is the inevitability of human mortality and the infinite wisdom of enjoying life and one's accomplishments. At one critical juncture, Siduri the barmaid advises Gilgamesh as follows.

> Gilgamesh, where do you roam?
> You will not find the eternal life you seek.
> When the gods created mankind
> They appointed death for mankind,
> Kept eternal life in their own hands.
> So, Gilgamesh, let your stomach be full,
> Day and night enjoy yourself in every way,
> Every day arrange for pleasures.
> Day and night, dance and play,
> Wear fresh clothes.
> Keep your head washed, bathe in water,
> Appreciate the child who holds your hand,
> Let your wife enjoy herself in your lap.[59]

When the Standard Babylonian Version of the Gilgamesh Epic was discovered, it created an international sensation, largely because of the eleventh of the twelve tablets and its story of the flood.[60] Although it is by no means certain that the Old Babylonian Version included the eleventh tablet, it might be helpful to include a comment here on this important portion of the Epic. On his quest for immortality, Gilgamesh learns of only one immortal man, Utnapishtim, who has been called the "Babylonian Noah." Gilgamesh is astonished to find, not a young and vigorous Utnapishtim, but an elderly man, for eternal youth had escaped him even if immortality had not. Utnapishtim explains how he achieved immortality when he was forewarned of a divine plan to flood the world. He survived the flood in a large reed boat accompanied by his family and pairs of all animals. Since, however, this event was unrepeatable, it gives Gilgamesh little hope for immortality. He himself fails three tests by which he could have received immortality. In defeat he resigns himself to the inevitability of death and takes comfort in his achievements. The remarkable parallels with Gen 6–9 have intrigued readers of the Bible since 3 December 1872, when George Smith announced his discovery and asserted that the Hebrew version was derived from the Babylonian.[61] Today it is more modestly assumed that the Israelite and Babylonian versions share a common source, since the later date for the Hebrew version does not necessitate direct borrowing from the Akkadian.

Indeed, traditions of a great flood assailing earth and humankind have a long history in Babylonian lore. As we saw in chapter 1, the beginnings of civilization in southern Mesopotamia were possible because of access to the life-giving waters of the Tigris and Euphrates Rivers and their many channels and streams. However, life in this rich alluvial plain was also tenuous because the rivers flooded almost every spring, prior to the building of diversionary dams in modern times.[62] Frequently in antiquity the Euphrates overflowed and spread across the plain to the Tigris, which itself at times overflowed. Because of topography, such floods did not occur in Syria-Palestine and Anatolia, making it likely that early Sumerian traditions have influenced the various flood stories of the ancient world.[63] The Sumerian King List preserves the tradition that one such flood was so catastrophic that it stood between the remote primordial past and more recent history, and we have a Sumerian flood story involving a single human survivor, Ziusudra.[64]

This Sumerian flood story has survived in copies from late in the Old Babylonian period and may have been the model or inspiration for the sequence of creation, antediluvian ancestors, and the flood in Genesis.[65] However, a more direct impact of the Old Babylonian "legacy" is contained in the Epic of Atra-ḫasis, dated to around 1700 B.C.E., although its actual composition may have been centuries earlier.[66] This epic also presents in sequence the creation of humanity and its near extinction in the flood. Before humans existed, the high gods forced the rest of the deities to perform manual labor. The lesser deities rebelled against this arrangement, and, as a result, one of their number was killed, and the high gods created humankind using his remains. Humans were thus created in order to assume the responsibility for undesirable physical work and to provide for the gods. Eventually humans also became vexatious to the high gods, who decided to destroy humankind in a massive flood. But one of the humans was warned in advance of the flood, and he survived in a boat. This one, Atra-ḫasis (whose name means "ultrawise") is the hero of the epic. We have many editions from various periods of Mesopotamian history, and one of these was expanded to provide the flood story of the eleventh tablet of Gilgamesh.

The most important nonliterary text from the Old Babylonian period is, of course, the Code of Hammurapi, the text of which is best preserved on an eight-foot diorite stela, now housed in the Louvre (see fig 3.5).[67] The monument was recovered in 1901 in Susa, where it had been taken from Babylon as a trophy of war by the Elamites in the thirteenth century B.C.E.,

Fig. 3.5. The stela of Hammurapi. The text is inscribed in columns in Neo-Sumerian style script. The iconography portrays the god Shamash seated on his altar, while Hammurapi stands reverentially before him. Location: Louvre, Paris, France. Photo Credit: Réunion des Musées Nationaux/Art Resource, NY.

probably from the temple of Shamash at Sippar. The text itself consists of an extensive prologue; 282 laws, most of which are well preserved; and an epilogue. The large collection of casuistic laws is the longest, best organized, and best attested from ancient Mesopotamia. References, in the prologue especially, to various cities and regions that Hammurapi claimed as part of his realm make it clear that this version of the Code was issued very late in his reign, probably around his thirty-ninth or fortieth year. The laws themselves are quite formulaic, but the prologue and epilogue are written in an elegant hymnic style often compared to earlier royal hymns, and they constitute some of the finest Old Babylonian literary style, often serving as the "show case" text for beginning students of Akkadian.

The Code's tripartite structure—prologue, laws, epilogue—and the nature of many of the laws in the Code show that in this, as in most other aspects of Old Babylonian culture available to us, the mystique of earlier Sumerian culture continued to hold powerful influence. This literary continuity between the Code and its predecessors in Babylonia (the Neo-Sumerian code and those from Isin and Eshnunna) implies that each "code" is, in fact, a modification of an already-existing body of laws and is in some sense actually a legal "reform." Some laws thus are traditional and are repeated almost word for word from previous codes, while others are newly constituted to meet the needs of the contemporary setting.[68]

The laws deal with nearly every possible situation in ancient Babylonian society, including criminal matters such as murder, robbery, assault, and bodily injuries, as well as civil matters such as real estate sales and rentals, marriage, inheritance, adoption, and the like. They are clearly meant to prescribe directives for the future in casuistic format (the hypothetical clause "If x occurs, then y shall be done"), although they are probably not genetically related to specific cases. We are not at all sure details in the Code reflect reality in ancient Babylonia rather than an idealized or artificial conception. Nonetheless, any investigation into Old Babylonian society must begin here. The laws speak often and clearly of three groups of individuals, which are often thought of as classes: *awīlum* ("man"), *muškēnum* ("crown dependent"?), and *wardum* ("slave"). We have not been able to determine the nature of the second category, how it differs from the first, and whether one became a *muškēnum* or was born into the position, despite intense investigation since the appearance of the Code over a century ago. Injuries to the *awīlum* were punishable by means of higher financial restitution than for injuries to the *muškēnum,* and it is possible we should think of the former as a "free citizen" and the *muškēnum* as some sort of crown dependent. Such dependents would have received land allotments in exchange for a fixed number of days of work per month or year. But it is not at all clear that the *muškēnum* belonged to a lower social stratum than the *awīlum*.[69]

Since it is the most extensive legal document prior to classical times, the Code has been the subject of an enormous corpus of scholarly literature. Topics of investigation have included the art and iconography of the investiture scene on the rounded top of the stela, the historical and religious information gleaned especially from the deities and cities mentioned in the prologue, and, of course, the questions raised by the laws them selves for the history of law. A perennial and perplexing question for legal historians has been, What precisely *is* the Code of Hammurapi? Despite conventional usage, which I have followed here, it is doubtful that it should even be called a "code," since certain types of legal cases are omitted from the list, and it is apparently intended to cover *most* situations without an attempt to be comprehensive. Furthermore, we have little evidence of their referential authority in a legal system or court specifically dependent upon them, although we have abundant evidence of such legal procedures, and it seems only logical to conclude that they were in fact dependent on the Code of Hammurapi during the Old Babylonian period.[70] It is clear that the Code is not the same as a royal *mīšarum* decree abolishing debts (see above). Perhaps it is only royal propaganda, a hymn of self-praise extolling the king's achievements but having little effect on the average Babylonian on the street.[71] Or perhaps it is an anthology of specific royal pronouncements on individual cases.[72] Interestingly, in the epilogue of the Code, Hammurapi includes his motivation for setting up the stela.

> In order that the mighty not wrong the weak, to provide just ways for the waif and the widow, I have inscribed my precious pronouncements upon my stela and set it up before the statue of me, the king of justice, … in order to render the judgments of the land, to give the verdicts of the land, and to provide just ways for the wronged.[73]

Hammurapi's twenty-second year-name contains a reference to an image of himself as "king of justice," which is likely the "statue" he mentions here. Apparently this impressive stela of laws was raised to stand beside another statue portraying the king as champion of justice, which he had raised nearly two decades earlier. Whatever practical uses the Code had, it at least also served an important role as royal propaganda, as this reference in the epilogue implies.

For readers of the Hebrew Bible, Hammurapi's list of casuistic laws contains great interest due to their many interesting parallels with Israelite law, found particularly in the "Book of the Covenant" (Exod 21–23), the Holiness Code (Lev 17–26), and the legal core of Deuteronomy (Deut 19–25). Some of the parallels are striking and have occupied scholars for decades. Moreover, the Code's continuity with its predecessors in the

Neo-Sumerian and Isin-Larsa periods makes it likely that the internal arrangement of the law collections throughout Babylonia was far from haphazard but followed clearly reasoned conceptual patterns, which are present in the biblical laws as well.[74] Thus the parallels between the Babylonian laws and those of the Bible are remarkable, both in specific details and in macrostructure.

Before leaving this discussion of the Code of Hammurapi, it may be of particular interest to readers of the Bible to consider recent speculation about these connections between Old Babylonian legal traditions and those of the Pentateuch. Closely shared legal traditions are not numerous, but a few are undeniable and need explanation. Some scholars argue for an Amorite "bridge" by which shared cultural features were transmitted,[75] while others assume a first-millennium B.C.E. association after Israel came into immediate contact with Mesopotamian culture.[76] Recently it has been suggested that two specific sets of laws may be identified as native to Amorite culture: debt release and the *lex talionis* (or "law of retaliation," i.e., the principle of "an eye for an eye, tooth for a tooth").[77] Talionic punishments have long been suspected as Amorite in origin,[78] but when combined with debt release (and perhaps others!), it is striking that these are shared features in the Babylonian and biblical laws but absent in much other legal material from the ancient world. In other words, the very laws that are most likely Amorite are also the ones shared most closely in the Bible and in the Code of Hammurapi. When investigating such links, rather than speak of a borrowing one from the other, or a transmission of one to the other, we may need to consider the possibility that both have their origins in the same rich Amorite tribal and seminomadic customs.

Another genre of Old Babylonian literature of interest as part of the period's legacy is a burgeoning prophetic literature (of particular interest to students of the Bible, for obvious reasons). "Prophecy" may be understood in this discussion as a branch of divination, in which the human prophet transmits divine messages as a mouthpiece for the deity. Other forms of divination used in the ancient Near East are inductive; that is, they employed methods based on systematic observations of the cosmos and their scholarly interpretations in order to deduce the divine will. Babylonia had a rich tradition in these inductive methods, too, such as extispicy (the most popular type of divination, which involved the inspection of sacrificial sheep entrails), hepatoscopy (liver omens), astral omens, and so forth. But most of these had been part of southern Mesopotamian culture since the Old Akkadian period.[79] Eventually, however, certain astrological omens were stripped of their protases (an opening conditional clause stating the proposition), leaving compilations of apodoses (the prediction itself), or literary prophecies.[80]

So apart from these other forms of divination, prophetic speech per se was first recorded in the Old Babylonian period, and some have suggested it was introduced by the Amorites.[81] Such prophetic speech is transmittive, involving a deity, a message, a human transmitter, and recipient(s).[82] The greatest majority of Old Babylonian prophetic texts are from Mari in the northwest, and another group comes from later Neo Assyrian sources. But occasionally we have prophetic texts from Babylonia proper, such as an oracle of the goddess Kititum (a regional manifestation of Ishtar) to King Ibalpiel of Eshnunna dated to the mid-eighteenth century B.C.E.

> O king Ibalpiel, thus says Kititum: The secrets of the gods are placed before me. Because you constantly pronounce my name with your mouth, I constantly disclose the secrets of the gods to you. On the advice of the gods and by the command of Anu, the country is given you to rule. You will ransom the upper and lower country, you will amass the riches of the upper and lower country. Your commerce will not diminish; there will be a permanent food of peace for any country that your hand keeps hold of. I, Kititum, will strengthen the foundations of your throne; I have established a protective spirit for you. May your ear be attentive to me![83]

Babylonian art, like its culture in general, is an interesting amalgamation of Sumerian and Semitic tastes and styles. The Babylonians used most of the same art forms and media of expression used throughout Mesopotamian history: cylinder seals, sculpture, metalwork, and the like. But each major period of Babylonian history brought its distinctive innovations. The Old Babylonian period witnessed the introduction of wall painting and minor changes in the traditional styles of cylinder seals. There is also evidence that artisans produced clay plaques in mass quantities and figurines early in the period, but otherwise they seemed to have continued the older Mesopotamian styles.[84]

Additionally, the Babylonians of this period made significant advances in fields we might call "scientific" endeavors, particularly mathematics and astronomy. Hundreds of multiplication and division tables as well as many problem texts from the Old Babylonian scribal school at Nippur manifest an impressive aptitude in mathematics during this period. The high level of algebraic achievement by the early Babylonians has led some to compare this period with the early Renaissance.[85] In addition to the decimal system familiar to Western culture (using powers of 10), Babylonian scholars also used a sexagesimal system (employing powers of 60) originally devised by the Sumerians and coming down to us in the form of the 60-minute hour and the 360-degree circle.

Babylonian astronomical observations date at least to the end of the Old Babylonian period. The so-called "Venus Tablets," a group of texts from the time of Ammi-saduqa, record the rising and setting of the planet

Venus during the early years of the king's reign.[86] These sightings provide three possible dates for Ammi-ṣaduqa's accession year, leaving us with "high" (1702), "middle" (1646), and "low" (1582) dates for his eighth year and fixing high, middle, and low chronologies. As stated in the preface, I have followed the middle chronology, which has become standard in Assyriology, although recent studies have brought all of this into question.[87] Though these early celestial observations were probably recorded for divination and religious motives, astronomy eventually distinguished itself from astrology as a separate science. As we shall see, scholars of the Neo-Babylonian period displayed an impressive ability to combine accurate astronomical observation with advanced mathematical calculation, resulting in a sophisticated lunar-solar calendar that was thoroughly predictable and free from mere observation.

In taking up the next topic in this discussion of Old Babylonian culture, that of religion, we encounter a dilemma. Is it possible to speak with confidence from our contemporary, Western perspective about religious beliefs and practices in ancient Babylonia? Scholars are not agreed on this point. Thorkild Jacobsen traced the history of Mesopotamian religion through four thousand years of development in which the gods were viewed first as providers for the necessities of life, then as protectors against enemies, next as parents with whom personal relationships were possible, and finally in the first millennium, as cruel warriors.[88] Many view this reconstruction as interesting but much too speculative. The opposite extreme argues that a Mesopotamian religion "cannot and should not be written" because of a lack of available evidence and, more seriously, because of the tremendous conceptual and cultural barriers that separate us from such an ancient polytheistic religion.[89] The elusive middle ground is possible to find, provided one remembers the limitations caused by the conceptual gulf between us and the ancient Babylonians.[90]

The Babylonian pantheon, numbering into the thousands, was an interesting blend of Sumerian and Semitic deities that were basically related to natural phenomena.[91] Most of the great gods of Babylonia were given Semitic names but were identical in character and function to their Sumerian counterparts: Anu, god of the heavens (Sumerian An); Enlil, king of the lands (who kept his Sumerian name); Ea, god of wisdom and magic whose dominion was the sweet-water ocean under the earth (Sumerian Enki). These three were grandfather, father, and son, respectively, and make up a cosmic triad of the greatest gods. Three other important deities are celestial in nature and also of the same family: Sîn, the moon god (Sumerian Nanna), was also father of Shamash, the sun god (Sumerian Utu), and Ishtar, goddess of the planet Venus (Sumerian Inanna). Under Semitic influence, this last deity, as goddess of both love and war, assimilated the personality and functions of other goddesses. Thus most aspects of nature, as it was perceived by Sumero-Babylonian scholars, were deified and systematized by the earliest theologians. With the growth of urbanization and the city-state culture in southern Mesopotamia, each god became the head of one city, so that all the major deities were honored, making it possible for Sumerian cities to benefit from mutual cooperation.[92] Most likely rivers, springs, and mountains were also deified in prehistoric times but gradually lost divine status in historical periods. Political events in the Old Babylonian period resulted in adoption and modification of this theological worldview. The process of convergence and location of divine attributes into fewer deities also began at this time, which will become important later.

In addition, there were Old Babylonian innovations in this pantheon. Adad, the weather god, was of secondary importance in Sumerian religion but rose to prominence during this period. Conversely, some important Sumerian deities are of lesser significance in the Babylonian pantheon (e.g., Tammuz [Sumerian Dumuzi]). Subsequently, as the city of Babylon rose politically in the second millennium, Marduk also rose to preeminence in the pantheon (see ch. 5 below). During the long history of Babylonia, religious developments may be described in two paradoxical trends. On the one hand, we can trace the proliferation of deities at the village and local cult setting; on the other hand, we have definite syncretism of many deities in specific cities and eventually in national pantheons.

These deities were sexual beings who married, raised families, and were subject to injury or even death. Humankind was created to relieve the gods from the burden of physical labor and to perform ritual service to the gods. Among such service was the provision of the deity's food, drink, and libation for his or her regular meals. The gods themselves prescribed the rituals in which they received portions of the sacrificial animals, the rest going to the king and temple officials. The king was perceived as the official representative of the deity, and it was his responsibility to ensure the fertility of the land through the careful observance of the New Year rituals. In the temples themselves, an elaborate priestly bureaucracy was responsible for maintaining the temple and its deity.[93]

The temple itself could spread over many acres and consist of several buildings. The dominant feature of the temple complex was the ziggurat, a stepped tower of three to seven stages. The precise role and function of these towers is still an open question. They may have been connected to the idea that gods originally lived in mountains and the ziggurat served as a substitute. More likely, the building of ziggurats evolved slowly in the history of Mesopotamian temple building. The earliest shrines were built on the ground, developing over time through stages using elevated platforms and eventually to the familiar stepped, rectangular pyramids with the shrine on top, raised above the rest of the city.[94] In the temple itself was the cella or long narrow chamber in which the god was housed. The divine statue was usually carved from wood, adorned with precious stones or metals, and stood on a raised platform or in a niche. The deity was actually thought to be present in its statue, which is borne out by a ritual performed soon after its manufacture. By this ritual (*mīs pî,* "mouth-washing"), the idol's mouth and eyes were symbolically opened and the "work of human hands" became the real presence of the deity, in a way sometimes compared to the Roman Catholic theology of the "Eucharistic Presence," in which the bread and wine become the real presence of the divine Jesus for Orthodox and Roman Catholics.[95]

The Babylonians saw the universe as a single closed system in which events in one realm mirrored those of another. So events in the human domain reflected events in the divine realm, and successive observable events in nature may be connected by a cause-and-effect relationship. There developed in Babylonia a "pseudoscience" for observing unusual natural phenomena and the events that followed them. It was assumed that this sequence could be repeated in the future. Thus through divination, the will of the gods could be determined and the future could be predicted. Many such omen techniques were practiced, such as the observation of animals' entrails, oil in water, smoke from incense, the behavior of birds, celestial phenomena, and so forth.

4

The Middle Babylonian Period

The next four and a half centuries of Babylonian history are not
marked by the rise and dominance of a world empire with Babylon at its
center. Nor is there any one particular ethnic component of the country,
which innervates and signals cultural changes, as the Amorites had done
in the first half of the second millennium. Rather, we need here to consider
ways in which the power vacuum in southern Mesopotamia was filled by
the Kassites after the collapse of the Old Babylonian Empire, the cultural
significance of Babylonia during these centuries of Kassite rule, and the
role it played in a new age of internationalism across the ancient Near East.
Although not entirely satisfying, I have followed the conventional nomenclature by calling this the Middle Babylonian period (1595–1155 B.C.E.).

4.1. The Fall of Babylon

The once expansive empire of the Old Babylonian period was reduced
considerably during the century and a half in which Hammurapi's five successors ruled Babylonia (1750–1595 B.C.E.). The northwestern territories
(formerly the kingdom of Mari) were lost to the new kingdom of Hana,
the north soon felt pressure from the Kassite newcomers, and a series of
uprisings in the south eventually resulted in losses to a dynasty that later
tradition would call the "First Sealand Dynasty."[1] The final blow to the
Amorite Dynasty at Babylon came from elsewhere, however: the Hittites,
Indo-Europeans from Anatolia. The Hittite Old Kingdom was just
expanding beyond its homeland (Ḫatti), and Murshili I (1620–1595 B.C.E.)
continued the policies of his predecessor with spectacular successes
against their traditional enemy in Syria, Aleppo. Having taken Aleppo and
securing his borders, Murshili continued down the Euphrates, motivated
presumably by the riches Babylon had to offer, and forged into Babylonia
encountering little resistance. He had, however, grossly overextended his
reach, since the Hittite kingdom was not prepared for administrative control of conquered territories so far from Ḫatti-land. After sacking the city of
Babylon in 1595, Murshili hastened home only to die in a palace conspiracy, and the Hittites withdrew leaving a political vacuum in Babylonia.[2]

Events immediately after the fall of Babylon are obscured by the dearth of documentary evidence, leading many scholars to refer to this period as a "dark age." Even the length of time between the fall of Babylon and the Kassite Dynasty is nebulous, making chronological precision impossible for second-millennium Mesopotamian history. Nevertheless, it is misleading to refer to this period as a "dark age," because this implies—in addition to the absence of written sources—a breakdown in civil order, widespread social disintegration, and economic ruin.[3] But this is distinctly not true of the Middle Babylonian period. As soon as the Kassite Dynasty exerted itself and brought stability to the region, writing soon reappeared as an important feature of the culture and continued to be important throughout most of the Middle Babylonian period, as we shall see. Although Babylonia had experienced some lack of societal cohesion and loss of economic progress toward the end of the First Dynasty of Babylon, such conditions did not persist under Kassite rule. Finally, if in fact the middle chronology should be abandoned in favor of the so-called low chronology, as has been argued recently, then the so-called "dark age" between Samsu-ditana and the Kassite Dynasty, with its fewer documentary sources, may have been briefer than we thought before.[4]

Thus, the four and a half centuries of the Middle Babylonian period are clearly demarcated by sociopolitical turning points in ancient Near Eastern history generally. On the one hand, at the beginning of the period, the hiatus between the fall of Babylon and the Kassite Dynasty, however long it may have lasted, breaks the three-thousand-year Mesopotamian tradition roughly in half.[5] The Old Babylonian period shares much in common with the rich traditions of the third millennium, while the Kassite Dynasty shares a certain "nationalism" that is new and more at home in the first millennium. While the Kassites will represent virtually no break from the Old Babylonian period *culturally,* important *political* differences will be obvious, reflecting the beginning of an internationalism that will change the course of ancient history permanently. On the other hand, the end of the Middle Babylonian period (generally the turn from Bronze to Iron Ages archaeologically, ca. 1200 B.C.E.) is marked by the collapse of major powers in the ancient world and the emergence of an altogether different political order, as we shall see in the next chapter.

4.2. THE KASSITE DYNASTY

The first beneficiaries of the Hittite raid on Babylon were the rulers of a dynasty from the so-called "Sealand" in the southern marshes of Babylonia.[6] The Sealand (Akkadian *māt tâmtim,* "land of the sea," *AHw* 1354, ¶6) was the first-millennium name for the extreme southern portions of Babylonia, at the head of the Persian Gulf. Here the Tigris and Euphrates emptied their waters into expansive marshlands, lagoons, and lakes, which may have reached much farther north in antiquity than today. Subsistence in the marshes was based, not on the cereal-cultivated agriculture of the rest of Babylonia, but on fishing, collecting reeds for matting and architecture, and perhaps the breeding of water buffalo, as today.[7] Life in these southern marshes was often isolated from political events in Babylonia, and its inhabitants were occasionally freedom-loving, independent types, who were controlled only by the most stable of dynasties in the north.

The dynasty of the Sealand traces its line back to the time of Hammurapi's son Samsu-iluna and apparently engaged him in warfare.[8] Little is known of the dynasty besides the royal names of its rulers, and their names imply they aspired to lead a revival of Sumerian culture in the south. After the Hittite withdrawal and an indefinite passage of time, the sixth dynast from the Sealand, Gulkishar, took northern Babylonia, holding the city of Babylon itself briefly. Although the Sealand Dynasty's hold on Babylon was ephemeral, it was able to hold off the Kassites in the north for a century or more. This accomplishment alone was enough to ensure a legacy, which is documented in the important historical text known as the Babylonian King List A.[9] This tablet, which unfortunately is damaged and contains many gaps, lists rulers from the First Dynasty of Babylon to the end of Assyrian rule around 600 B.C.E. The list details successive claimants to the throne of Babylon, which served as a figurative capital for the respective dynasties, including a note identifying each dynasty (*palû*) and the total number of kings and length of duration for each dynasty. After six more rulers, the Sealand Dynasty fell to the Kassites, who now were strong enough to hold all of Babylonia.

During the first half of the second millennium, Amorite city-states of various sizes had slowly but decisively supplanted the older Sumero-Akkadian culture. The second half of the millennium was dominated by a different ethnic element in Mesopotamia, the Kassites. Their own name for themselves, *galzu,* was akkadianized as *kaššû,* the origin of Greek *kossaioi* and of our name for them.[10] But there were many other ethnolinguistic groups in the country at this time, and, in fact, during the last three and a half centuries of the second millennium Babylonia proper was something of a melting pot. In addition to an amalgamation of older Amorite stock—now the "Babylonians"—other groups in significant numbers included Assyrians, Elamites, Hurrians, Lullubi, and the Aḫlamū, who were precursors of the Arameans.[11]

The Kassites themselves had appeared as foreign invaders in western Babylonia prior to the fall of Babylon to the Hittites.[12] The original Kassite homeland is unknown, although it is often assumed they migrated from Iran through the Zagros Mountains. We possess no connected text in the Kassite language, knowledge of which is limited to bilingual lists of personal names and deity names, revealing a language that appears to be unrelated to any other and little understood by the Babylonian scribes.[13] Considering the length and importance of the Kassite Dynasty, we have relatively little archaeological evidence to help. Yet they established a ruling family that remained in power (with few interruptions) for almost four hundred years, the longest continuously ruling dynasty in Babylonian history.[14] Paradoxically, so little is known of the specifics of their reign, especially due to a lack of primary sources, that we have no comprehensive survey of their political history in English.[15]

How the Kassites came to power is beyond the grasp of historical reconstruction. They first appear in northern Babylonia as early as the eighteenth century B.C.E., as seminomadic groups in the countryside, serving as farm workers or military mercenaries, and occasionally appearing as threatening attackers.[16] From settled regions in the northeast near the Tigris, they expanded westwards, appearing sporadically in locations across northwestern Mesopotamia and briefly establishing a small kingdom at Terqa along the Euphrates. For approximately two centuries of early Kassite history, we are unable to know more than this (hence scholars are prone to refer to a "dark age"). From positions of strength along the Euphrates, especially at Terqa in Hana, the Kassites might have been able to block Murshili's march on Babylon in 1595, but for reasons unknown to us, they did not.

As we have seen, sometime after the Hittite retreat from Babylon (remembering that the chronology is obscure), Gulkishar took northern Babylonia and established the Sealand Dynasty's legacy in subsequent Babylonian lore. However, around 1475 B.C.E., led by a king named Ulam-Buriash, the Kassites responded by driving the Sealand rulers back to the south and unifying most of Babylonia (which they called Kar-Duniash) into a single Kassite Dynasty. The Sealand Dynasty was for a while limited to the southern marshes, but even this last remnant of resistance was brought into the Kassite state by the end of the fifteenth century.

As frustrating as it is to have so few details relating to the beginning of the Kassite Dynasty, our situation does not improve when trying to reconstruct events over the next few centuries. Besides our lack of primary sources, historians are plagued further by the tendency among Kassite rulers to use the same throne names, making it difficult to place the few dated texts we have in the proper reign with confidence. This problem is compounded by the Kassite practice (after approximately the fourteenth century B.C.E.) of dating legal and administrative texts by regnal years rather than the use of year-names, which were so helpful in reconstructing events of the Old Babylonian period.[17] So a system of dating by regnal year, assigning each year a number of a king's rule—such as "the first year of Kurigalzu," "the second year of Kurigalzu," and so on—became standard in Babylonia beginning with the Kassites of the fourteenth century B.C.E. and continued in use among the several dynasties until the third century B.C.E. Although the regnal-year system provides a helpful framework for reconstructing the chronology of ancient Babylonia generally, it does not identify what was considered the most important event of each year as the system of year-names had done. Additionally, even the task of establishing a list of Kassite kings is difficult.[18] Of course, chronology continues to be a problem, especially for the early periods.

Despite these limitations, we are able to determine that the Kassite rulers established a new capital on a hill approximately nineteen miles west of modern Baghdad at the point where the Tigris and Euphrates rivers run closest together (see fig. 4.1).[19] Toward the end of the fifteenth or beginning of the fourteenth century B.C.E., King Kurigalzu I expanded an older settlement at the site and named it Dur-Kurigalzu ("Fort of Kurigalzu"), leaving Babylon to be a ceremonial and religious capital. We can only imagine what motives compelled the Kassites to build the new capital, but its location may have protected important trade routes or guarded against imperialistic tendencies of Assyria in the north or Elam in the west. The site, which has never been thoroughly excavated, is dominated by a ziggurat, worn to its core, revealing fascinating details of its construction of reed-matting and bitumen between mud-brick layers.[20]

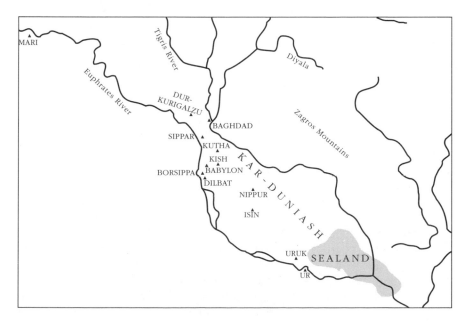

Fig. 4.1. Kassite Babylonia.

Although never dominant militarily, the Kassites were generally successful at defending their borders by concluding treaties with Assyria and
Egypt and by using nonmilitary means of diplomacy with other potential
enemies. Through these diplomatic efforts they brought political stability
to southern Mesopotamia unlike anything known in the Old Babylonian
period. Occasional military threats were posed by Assyria to the north
and Elam to the east, and Kassite forces were engaged in border skirmishes with these enemies. Assyria under Tukulti-Ninurta I (1243–1207
B.C.E.) actually conquered Babylonia, sacked the city, and used Assyrian
governors to rule Babylon for seven years.[21] Ultimately, however, the fall
of the Kassite Dynasty was related to the devastation and collapse of other
states at the end of the Bronze Age, including the Hittites in Anatolia, several states along the Levantine coast, Mycenaean Greece and Cyprus
further east, and the loss to Egypt of its holdings in Syria-Palestine, all of
which caused population displacements and chaos throughout the ancient
Near East (the causes for which, see ch. 5). In the new political climate,
power in western Asia shifted from the Mediterranean basin in the west to
Assyria and Elam in the east.[22] After struggling against Assyria for decades,
the real threat to Kassite Babylonia became Elam toward the end of the
thirteenth century B.C.E. A series of Elamite raids into Babylonia culminated
in a devastating invasion by Shutruk-Nahhunte I of Elam around 1158
B.C.E.[23] It was likely at this time that the Elamites captured and deported
the stela of Hammurapi's law code and statues of the deities Marduk and
Sarpanitum, his consort. The Kassite king, Enlil-nadin-aḫḫe, led a rebellion
in response, but the Elamites killed him in 1155 B.C.E. and brought the Kassite period to an end.[24]

4.3. THE AGE OF INTERNATIONALISM

The defeat of the Sealand around 1475 under Ulam-Buriash and subsequent unification of all Babylonia may be said to be a turning point in
Babylonian history. By the close of the fifteenth century B.C.E., the Kassites
had incorporated even the Sealand regions of the south into their domain,
and the era of city-states was officially over. From this point forward, the
Kassite ruler was no longer "King of Sumer and Akkad" but rather "King
of Babylonia," ruler of a unified state—from Baghdad to Basra, we might
say. Perhaps the single greatest accomplishment of the Kassite Dynasty
was the formation of a national monarchy with clearly defined borders similar to the geographical reach of Hammurapi's brief empire. But the
Kassites maintained the whole region as a single political identity over centuries of time in a region notorious for political fragmentation. From this
point forward, Babylonia will remain a united political entity, even when
conquered and controlled by outside forces, and indeed, it is now entirely

appropriate to speak of southern Mesopotamia as "Babylonia," whereas prior to this point it was—strictly speaking—anachronistic.[25]

This new political unification, with centralized administration and societal stability, resulted in an impressive period of prosperity and affluence for Babylonia.[26] Excavations at the ancient city of Nippur yielded an archive from this period (mostly still unpublished) revealing an administrative system that brought considerable revenue to the state. We also have evidence of an efficient taxation system, levied on agricultural produce, provincial travel, and the requirement of corvée labor for building projects. As an important crossroads for trade throughout the ancient Near East, Kassite Babylonia exported textiles and manufactured goods, as well as horses and chariotry as part of its breeding industry, and became an essential passageway for jewelry and lapis lazuli (from Iran in the east). In return, Babylonia received valuable commodities often lacking in southern Mesopotamia (metals, wood, and precious stones), particularly enormous amounts of gold from Egypt's Nubian mines. During and after the Amarna period (below), the country actually used gold as the standard of equivalence rather than the traditional silver.[27] Kassite rulers devoted this considerable wealth to the country's infrastructure and architecture, both religious and royal. All the major cities of the country were repaired or expanded under their rule.

In a sense, the nationalistic impulse was not unique to southern Mesopotamia. A new age was dawning across the ancient Near East during the Late Bronze Age, in which nation states were emerging, each with ambitious interests in trade and expansion. Along the Mediterranean coastal rim, Egypt and the Hittites of Anatolia were powerful entities, and they frequently bickered over the right to control the rich city-states of the Levant. Across Syria-Mesopotamia in the north, the Hurrians (biblical "Horites") occupied much territory and were forged into a state by foreign, Indo-European rulers, who gave their name to the country: Mitanni. Eventually the Assyrians began to emerge in northern Mesopotamia toward the end of this period, and the Elamites in the east.

The stability and prosperity of Kassite rule resulted in a literary fluorescence, as we shall see below. In general, the period brought an increase in the status and prestige of Babylonian professions, especially the writing craft, which became the privilege of the educated elite and accessible mostly to the wealthy.[28] The prestige and appreciation for all the Babylonian "sciences" spread beyond the borders of Kassite Babylonia to other parts of the ancient Near East, and Babylonian became the *lingua franca* of the day. The archive of cuneiform tablets found in 1887 at El-Amarna in Egypt contained 382 tablets, most of which were written in Babylonian. The majority of the texts are letters between Pharaohs Amenophis III and Amenophis IV (= Akhenaten) and the rulers of

Mitanni, Babylonia, Hittite Anatolia, Assyria, Alashiya (Cyprus), and the
Syro-Palestinian city-states over a thirty-year period (approximately 1385–
1355 B.C.E.).[29] This archive of diplomatic correspondence brilliantly illu-
minates the closing stages of a remarkable international age (sometimes
the "Amarna age") and reveals the esteem in which Babylonian literature, education, and culture were held among all the nations of the
ancient world.

In addition to the cultural esteem of Babylonia during this period,
the Amarna letters also provide insight into the diplomatic and political
position of Kassite Babylonia among the great powers of the age. Over
three hundred of the letters came into the Egyptian court from their
imperial holdings in the Levant, in which vassal rulers of the Canaanite
city-states routinely referred to the pharaoh as "my lord" and whose language often included obsequious but imploring tones. By contrast, in
the forty-three letters from the "Great Powers Club" (of which Kassite
Babylonia was one), the kings of the nations referred to each other as
"brothers," reflecting the metaphor of a small village community.[30]
Diplomatically arranged marriages were intended to seal consanguinity
among the Great Kings, such as the marriage of the daughter of the Kassite king Kadashman-Enlil I to Amenophis III.[31] These letters also
illustrate the mutually beneficial commerce between the great powers,
so that Kassite rulers provided horses, much desired chariots, and lapis
lazuli in exchange for Egypt's gold. Letters from Burna-Buriash II
(1375–1347 B.C.E.) reveal a king who did not hesitate to complain bitterly
about mistreatment (in his view) by Akhenaten, who allegedly provided
only five carriages to escort the Babylonian king's daughter to her wed-
ding in Egypt, or to be upset that Akhenaten sent no condolences to him
during a recent illness.[32] Burna-Buriash also protested against the Egyptian's negotiations with the Assyrians, claiming that Kassite Babylonia
was the overlord of Assyria.[33]

4.4. CULTURAL DEVELOPMENTS IN KASSITE BABYLONIA

Members of the Kassite ruling dynasty used mostly Kassite names,
which were quite distinctive compared to Akkadian names. Remarkably,
this is nearly the *only* foreign feature of their dynasty. The Kassites so
completely adopted the traditional Sumero-Akkadian culture inherited
from the Old Babylonian period that today we have a difficult time identifying the degree of "foreignness" in Kassite Babylonia.[34] Whether we
turn to scribal practices, language, literature, royal titulary and ideology,
or religious and cultic institutions, we are astounded by how nearly complete was the acculturation of the Kassite rulers to Babylonian culture.[35]
Thus we may speak of reconstructing, however sketchily, the history of

Kassite Babylonia during the Late Bronze Age, but we are in no position to write a history of the Kassite people.

As we have seen, we possess practically nothing in the Kassite language, only a Kassite-Babylonian vocabulary list, a brief Kassite name list with Babylonian equivalents, a few Kassite entries in Akkadian lexical texts, proper names embedded in Akkadian texts, and scattered words related to animal husbandry and a few other isolated terms in Akkadian contexts.[36] We have neither texts nor even sentence scraps written in Kassite. On the other hand, it is fortunate for us that Kassite rulers promoted traditional Babylonian literature and culture, so that the considerable intellectual achievements of previous generations were preserved. We have every indication that scribal arts flourished in the Middle Babylonian period, especially at Nippur and Ur. Scribal "families" (most likely professional "houses" rather than kinship groups) emerged in this period, devoted to particular Babylonian traditions and specializations, and later scribes of the first millennium B.C.E. often traced their lineage to famous fifteenth- and fourteenth-century ancestors, the founders of these scribal families, who were likely Babylonian scholars of the Kassite period.[37]

Middle Babylonian scribes concerned themselves largely with systematic collection, preservation, and, to a lesser degree, expansion of their Babylonian literary heritage. Included in these scribal activities was the creation of reference works based on the older genres of omens and magical literature, composition of medical and astrological compendia, and the like. As the scholars of the Old Babylonian period had preserved the Sumerian literary heritage, so now the Middle Babylonian scholars preserved Akkadian (or traditional Babylonian) literature in a process that may be compared to canonization.[38] So the Old Babylonian version of the Gilgamesh Epic (see ch. 3) was probably shaped into what became the Standard Version during the Kassite period, although it is known to us largely in copies of the seventh century B.C.E. (Ashurbanipal's library at Nineveh). Thus, the Middle Babylonian period may be considered the time when Babylonian literature "took on more or less stable forms."[39] The unified Kassite state and Babylonia's leadership role in the international community during this time may further explain why the widest geographical distribution of copies of the Gilgamesh Epic occurred in the late second millennium B.C.E.[40]

Preservation of "classical" Babylonian literature was not the only contribution of scholars in the Kassite period. Although precise dates for composition of such texts is impossible to determine, it is likely that Babylonia's most thorough treatment of theodicy was composed at this time, known traditionally by its first line *ludlul bēl nēmeqi* ("Let me praise the Lord of Wisdom").[41] The Sumerians had developed many wisdom types such as proverbs, maxims, precepts, and disputes. *Ludlul* is a profound philosophical poem, dealing with themes familiar to readers of the Hebrew Bible (especially the book of Job). The righteous narrator was abandoned by the gods, opposed by the king, victimized by the courtiers, afflicted with diseases, and finally rejected as a social outcast. After obtaining no

Fig. 4.2. The Flood Tablet, relating part of the Epic of Gilgamesh.
Dated to the seventh century B.C.E., from Nineveh, this is
perhaps the most famous cuneiform tablet from Mesopotamia.
© Copyright The British Museum.

relief from ·the clergy in charge of exorcism, the sufferer discovers the source of his trouble. It was not the king or the courtiers who were responsible, but Marduk himself. In a series of dreams, the pious hero learns that Marduk's wrath has been appeased, and his fortunes immediately begin changing. This "Babylonian Job" (as the author, Shubshi-meshre-Shakkan is sometimes called) may reflect a new theme of pessimism and resignation prominent in Kassite society,[42] due largely to changes in social setting and life experiences when compared to Old Babylonian times, where there was more structure and security for the middle classes.[43] Although many assume the Babylonian Epic of Creation (*Enūma Eliš,* "When on high") was also composed at this time, I shall reserve discussion of it for the next chapter for reasons explained there.

We know next to nothing about distinctive Kassite religion. In Kassite-Babylonian vocabulary and various lists mentioned earlier, we can identify the names of approximately two dozen gods in the Kassite pantheon.[44] However, we have no evidence that any of these deities were objects of worship at cult centers in Babylonia or were syncretized with previously existing cult centers. The only exceptions are Shuqamuna and Shumaliya, the protective gods of the Kassite royal family, whose shrine in Babylon was the site of royal investiture. Otherwise we have to assume that, as with other features of their culture, the Kassites adopted traditional Babylonian theology without change. In fact, it appears the kings eagerly promoted the traditional Babylonian cults. The degree to which this is true is evident in the new capital city Dur-Kurigalzu built in the early fourteenth century B.C.E. on the outskirts of modern Baghdad. The new city contained temples dedicated to prominent Sumerian deities and is dominated by a traditional stepped tower (ziggurat) like those of older Sumerian cities. It appears the Kassite rulers erected and repaired shrines only for the traditional Mesopotamian deities rather than deities of their own pantheon.[45]

One interesting innovation of Kassite Babylonia was a system of social organization that resulted in a new literary genre and a new royal practice. The literary genre is preserved on conically shaped boundary stones (Akkadian *kudurru,* "boundary, boundary stone")[46] standing approximately two feet, and erected to record and commemorate royal land grants (see fig. 4.3).[47] The stones were often inscribed with details about the plot of land, its dimensions, the taxes due, and a list of witnesses. Each *kudurru* usually contained a curse invoked against the one who tampers with the monument or deprives the owner of the land, and they usually also have symbols of deities on the top or side for extra apotropaic effect.[48] The new royal practice was the system in which the king granted to faithful subjects—family members, temple officials, priests, military officers, courtiers, and so forth—large parcels of land. This Kassite system is sometimes compared to medieval European feudalism or, more cautiously, "quasi-feudalism." However, it is doubtful whether this designation is appropriate for Kassite Babylonia since it anachronistically raises the wrong images for society in the second millennium B.C.E. Recently, significant differences have been outlined between the Kassite practices and true feudalism. Most importantly, the Kassite royal land grants attested on the *kudurru* stones, unlike feudalism, had little impact economically on the society at large, and they appear to represent the king's whimsical bestowal of favor.[49] We would be better served to abandon altogether the feudalistic descriptions of Kassite society.

It may also be observed that the material arts represent further Kassite innovations beyond those noted for the *kudurru* boundary stones. Although the evidence is slight and hardly conclusive, scenes on cylinder seals and, to a lesser degree, architectural remains reflect distinctive Kassite tastes and styles. New techniques of glass-working were developed so that larger quantities of glass were in use.[50]

In conclusion, the Kassites were only one of numerous ethnolinguistic groups of the Middle Bronze age in Mesopotamia, and it seems likely they would have disappeared forever from our records had it not been for one fact. They were ready and able to fill the power vacuum created by Murshili's abrupt return to Ḫatti-land after his raid on Babylon in 1595 B.C.E., making it possible for the Kassites to assume control and set the course of history for the next four centuries.[51] Their subsequent nationalism, with its stable economic and political rule, thus resulted also in the elevation of Babylonian culture and prestige across the ancient world in an age of internationalism and down through the pages of history.

Fig. 4.3. Boundary stone.
© Copyright The British Museum.

5

THE EARLY NEO-BABYLONIAN PERIOD

The sociopolitical history of Babylonia during the centuries following the collapse of the Kassite Dynasty is complex. We have no single political entity or royal dynasty conveniently holding the period together chronologically. Furthermore, we will encounter several people groups of diverse ethnic and regional backgrounds, beginning from the mid-twelfth century to approximately 800 B.C.E., making it difficult to discern a continuity in political developments. However, the *cultural* history of Babylonia during this period is not as complex and will be summarized at the conclusion of this chapter.

My use of "*early* Neo-Babylonian" may need explanation. The phrase is defensible on sociopolitical, cultural, and, somewhat less so, linguistic grounds. The designation "Neo-Babylonian" is regularly—and rightly—reserved for the dynastic rule of Nabopolassar and his successors in the late seventh and much of the sixth centuries B.C.E. (ch. 6), an empire built largely on the ruins of the Neo-Assyrian Empire. However, the Babylonian dialect of Akkadian took a distinct turn toward the beginning of the first millennium,[1] and although the country was not long unified or self-governed during these many centuries, a certain cultural uniformity is apparent, which is itself more akin to the first millennium than to the second. Thus *early* Neo-Babylonian in this context will refer to the period from the fall of the Kassites (1155 B.C.E.) to the rise of the Chaldeans in southern Babylonia (approximately 800 B.C.E.).[2]

5.1. "SEA PEOPLES" AND THE COLLAPSE OF BRONZE AGE CULTURE

The ancient Near East witnessed dramatic political changes around 1200 B.C.E., especially in the west along the Mediterranean rim. These changes are reflected in the archaeological designations "Bronze Age" and "Iron Age" used most commonly for Syro-Palestinian archaeology (see fig. 1.2 on p. 8). The demise of Bronze Age culture coincides with the collapse of the dominant empires of the Mediterranean world, the Hittites of Asia Minor and the Mycenaean civilization on the mainland of Greece, as well as most of the city-state polities in the Levant. Within a fifty-year period at the turn from the thirteenth to the twelfth centuries B.C.E., nearly every city in the eastern Mediterranean world collapsed in ways that appear from archaeological and textual evidence to have been rather sudden and cataclysmic. Egypt survived the carnage, although the New Kingdom came to an end and pharaonic dominance in Syria-Palestine was never the same. The twelfth century B.C.E. thus marks the beginning of hundreds of years of political struggle and uncertainty in the eastern Mediterranean. Indeed, events of this period may justifiably be called "the worst disaster in ancient history," comparable to the collapse of the western Roman Empire.[3]

These political events, marking the transition from Bronze to Iron Ages, were also accompanied by new cultural developments. The age of internationalism was officially over, and the Babylonian dialect ceased to be used as the *lingua franca*. A more convenient form of writing, the alphabet, spread beyond the Levant and changed the accessibility of written communication. New political systems began to emerge, especially in Syria-Palestine, where the political order which had existed for over three hundred years dissolved, and within a century new ethnic entities emerged in the vacuum in the form of the Aramean city-states of Syria and the Israelites and Philistines in the southern Levant. Eventually a new sense of nationalism began to emerge in certain of these political entities,[4] as did monotheistic impulses in places.

The first causes of these political and cultural developments are difficult to discern. In the 1870s, the Egyptologist Gaston Maspero formulated a theory on the basis of iconographical and inscriptional evidence from the time of Ramesses III (ca. 1187–1156 B.C.E.) that has had enormous influence on historians over the past century and a quarter. In Maspero's theory, at least four or five nations were forced out of Asia Minor and temporarily became nations of the sea, or "Sea Peoples": the Tursha, the Shardana, the Shekelesh, the Zakkala, and the Peleset (Philistines).[5] In point of fact, other texts from this period mention many such groups on the move across the Mediterranean, which are never referred to by a singular label, and the designation "Sea Peoples" is entirely Maspero's invention. His reliance on the nineteenth-century *Völkerwanderungstheorie,* postulating mass migrations as an explanation of national origins, makes the "Sea Peoples" hypothesis less than entirely satisfying as an explanation of the collapse of the Late Bronze Age culture. A distinction should be made between the concept of folk migrations as national entities, on the one hand, which appears now to be pure romantic fiction, and, on the other hand, the immigration of dozens of small groups from the Aegean, who certainly flowed into the Levant during this period. Our understanding of these people groups is still limited, but it is possible we should view them as raiders hoping to sack royal centers rather than as mass folk migrations seeking land on which their nations could settle.[6]

If the destruction of urban life across the eastern Mediterranean and the collapse of Bronze Age culture can no longer be satisfactorily explained as a result of bellicose "Sea Peoples" migrating into the region, what then is the alternative? A number of possibilities have been suggested, including natural catastrophes (e.g., earthquakes, drought, and famine), technological innovations (i.e., the invention of ironworking), shifts in patterns of production resulting in systems collapse, or simple piracy.[7] It seems likely a variety of factors converged near the beginning of the twelfth century B.C.E. to result in these profound changes in the ancient Near East. Although the arrival of thousands of Aegean newcomers undoubtedly played a significant role, it is simplistic to credit the changes to their arrival alone, and until new evidence becomes available, we must be content with an incomplete picture of the causes involved.

With these limitations of our available information in view, it is nevertheless quite clear that the political realities of the ancient Near East changed radically. With the collapse of the Hittites and Egyptians in the west, the center of power shifted to the east, especially Assyria, Babylonia, and Elam.[8] Babylonia itself remained relatively stable and experienced little impact from the carnage in Anatolia and the Mediterranean rim. The transition from the Kassite Dynasty to the Second Dynasty of Isin (see below) was precipitated by military pressure, ruralization and population decline in the urban centers, a westward shift in the Euphrates, and, possibly, other climatic changes.[9] On the other hand, the dominolike effect of the events in the eastern Mediterranean probably led to the arrival of the Arameans in central and southern Mesopotamia. Their everincreasing prominence contributed to the temporary decline of Assyria at the end of the twelfth century B.C.E.,[10] and by the beginning of the first millennium Arameans controlled not only southern Syria but the western territories of Babylonia.

Perhaps the most important factor contributing to the decline in southern Mesopotamia itself was the dramatic westward shift of the Euphrates River during the late Kassite period or shortly afterward. The gradual and sustained effects of salinization combined with the sudden shift of hydrological resources, resulting in devastation especially for cities of the northern alluvial plain.[11] Throughout Babylonia, the surrounding countryside gave way to pressure from tribal groups, as we shall see, and most of the cities were drastically reduced in population and in economic strength. As one follows the Euphrates River from north to south along a southeasterly direction, the decline in urbanism becomes less pronounced, presumably because the river gradually returns to a position close to its original course near Uruk and Ur. All of this resulted in a particularly susceptible northern Babylonia at the turn of the first millennium B.C.E.

In addition, a new threat to Babylonia's north emerged at this time and played an important roll throughout the next phase of Babylonian history. Assyria had appeared during the age of internationalism in the mid-fourteenth century B.C.E. under Ashur-uballiṭ I (1363–1328), growing already at that early stage into a territorial state.[12] The garrulous Burna-Buriash, king of the Kassites (see ch. 4) had protested vigorously when Assur-uballit asserted Assyria in an effort to gain equal standing among the Great Powers of the fourteenth century.[13] A few decades later, Shalmaneser I (1274–1245) led Assyria into new dominance throughout upper Mesopotamia, bringing under Assyrian control rich agricultural areas as well as trade routes to the Levant. The rise of Assyria continued unabated under Shalmaneser's son and successor, Tukulti-Ninurta I (1244–1208 B.C.E.), who ultimately clashed with Kassite Babylonia. As we noted in the previous chapter, Tukulti-Ninurta conquered Babylon and brought king Kashtiliash IV to Ashur in chains. The victory over Babylonia was celebrated in an elaborate epic poem,[14] and Tukulti-Ninurta assumed grandiose titles such as "king of the four shores."

Tukulti-Ninurta's conquest of Babylon in 1235 B.C.E. was short-lived and did not establish a prolonged period of Assyrian rule in Babylonia. But this event is interesting for two other reasons. First, it can be said to mark the beginning of Assyro-Babylonian conflict, which together with occasional Elamite involvement will characterize Mesopotamian history for the next several centuries. Second, it marks the beginning of significant Babylonian cultural influence on Assyria. In addition to dragging the Kassite ruler back to Ashur, the Assyrians also exiled Babylonian scribes and cuneiform tablets. Babylonia was the older and more sophisticated culture, especially when compared to the relatively provincial Assyria. Indications of Babylonian literary influence and religious dominance in Assyria reveal the interesting love-hate relationship that Assyria would develop with Babylonia for the next several centuries.

5.2. "Babylonia for the Babylonians"

The three centuries after the fall of the Kassites were marked by a succession of several dynasties featuring native Babylonian rulers. These rulers were "native" in the sense that they were not *recently* migrated to Mesopotamia; they were an amalgamation of various ethnic components that were by now indistinguishable.[15] In fact, this seems to be unique in the history of Babylonia, being the only period when native Babylonians controlled the country instead of foreign dynasties. By contrast, the Amorites built the Old Babylonian Empire, the Kassites were dominant during the Middle Babylonian period, and the Chaldeans in the Neo-Babylonian. Thus, this era (1158–812 B.C.E.) might reasonably be called "Babylonia for the Babylonians."[16]

The first successor to the Kassites is known as the "Second Dynasty of Isin," because the initial kings of the dynasty traced family origins back to Isin, the site of a powerful dynasty earlier in the second millennium.[17] This dynasty ruled Babylonia from 1157 to 1026 B.C.E. Although the Babylonian King List A is incomplete for this dynasty, it may be supplemented with royal economic and chronographic texts, which make it possible to reconstruct a list of names and approximate dates for eleven of the dynasts (see fig. 5.1).[18] During the early years of this dynasty, the Elamites to the east continued to plague northern Babylonia. But the fortunes of Babylonia changed with the fourth dynast, Nebuchadnezzar I (1125–1104 B.C.E.). He was the first of three or four Mesopotamian kings to bear this distinguished name, and care must be used to avoid confusing this king with the better-known Nebuchadnezzar II (605–562 B.C.E.) of the Neo-Babylonian Empire and one or perhaps two usurpers during the Persian period.[19] An additional word may be in order here on the variations of our Anglicized spellings of the well-known name. It comes down to us in two spellings (as here, and "Nebuchadrezzar" with *r*) because of the prominent role played by Nebuchadnezzar II in biblical traditions and because those traditions include both spellings in Biblical Hebrew. The Akkadian form, Nabû-kudurrī-uṣur, "O Nabû, protect my heir,"[20] is more technically correct as preserved in the spelling with *r*: *nĕbûkadre'ṣṣar,* Nebuchadrezzar (as it appears in Jeremiah and Ezekiel). The form with *n, nĕbûkadne'ṣṣar,* Nebuchadnezzar, occurs more frequently in the Hebrew Bible (2 Kings, 1 and 2 Chronicles, Ezra, Nehemiah, Esther, Jeremiah, and Daniel), and due largely to the beloved stories of the book of Daniel, where the name is spelled with *n,* this spelling has become more widely used as the standardized spelling and is the one I have chosen to use here.

Fig. 5.1. Selected Rulers of Babylon during the Early Neo-Babylonian Period

Nebuchadnezzar I (1125–1104)

***

Nabu-apla-iddina (888–855)
Marduk-zakir-shumi I (854–?)

***

Merodach-Baladan II (721–710)

***

Ashur-nadin-shumi (699–694)

Nebuchadnezzar I left an indelible mark on successive generations by avenging the Elamite sack of Babylon. The Elamites had taken the Marduk statue captive as a symbol of victory when they defeated the Kassites and continued to hold it in their capital city, Susa. Nebuchadnezzar launched a surprise attack during the heat of midsummer, reaching Susa and recovering the Marduk statue. The Elamites had been a constant threat to Babylonia, but they were of little consequence for the next three centuries. Nebuchadnezzar's victory restored the national morale of Babylonia, and the statue was returned to its shrine in Babylon accompanied by popular rejoicing. As an important religious consequence of this event, Marduk achieved a new level of supremacy in the Babylonian pantheon. This once relatively insignificant deity had assumed an increasingly visible role since the Old Babylonian period. He had a privileged position in the Old Babylonian pantheon, although he appears subordinate to Anu and Enlil in the prologue to the Code of Hammurapi.[21] On boundary stones and dedicatory inscriptions of the Kassite period, he continued to occupy a subordinate position. But one text from the time of Nebuchadnezzar I calls Marduk *šar ilāni,* "king of the gods," and from this time forward his kingship over the gods is commonly attested. Nebuchadnezzar's dramatic recovery of the Marduk statue appears now to have elevated him to the position of supreme deity, which was a reflex in the direction of monotheism appearing elsewhere in the ancient Near East at this time.[22]

The remainder of the Second Dynasty of Isin is less well attested. After several years of border skirmishes with Assyria, these two countries directed their attention to a common threat: Aramean groups who were invading Babylonia and Assyria from the west during a time of general famine.[23] The final dynasts left few original sources, and little is known about the last phase of the dynasty or about the circumstances surrounding the fall of the Second Dynasty of Isin. It seems likely that the Aramean invasions in the northwest weakened and eventually toppled the ruling dynasty. These encroachments from the northwest must have been a factor in determining that the next regime would be associated with the Sealand in the south.[24]

Over the next half century, Babylonia was ruled by a succession of three brief and undistinguished dynasties: the Second Sealand Dynasty (1026–1006 B.C.E.) ruled from the south; the Bazi Dynasty (1005–986 B.C.E.) was comprised of three Kassite tribal rulers; and the so-called Elamite Dynasty (985–980 B.C.E.) managed only a single dynast.[25] For the next century and a half, Babylonian political history is marked by two features: continued Aramean infiltration and the important relationship with Assyria to the north. The Arameans disrupted internal stability, making a powerful political base impossible. The relationship with Assyria would dominate Babylonian history for the next several centuries.

The political instability is apparent from the paucity of documentary evidence from the years 979–811 B.C.E. The Babylonian King List A is too fragmentary to detail the sequence of kings for Babylonia at this time.[26] Dynastic affiliations of the succeeding rulers of Babylon are impossible to outline for this period.[27] For most of the tenth century, Babylonia was marked by an east-west orientation. Aramean tribal groups kept the west in a constant state of disruption and controlled the important trade route along the Euphrates, while the sparse evidence available suggests that Babylonia's orientation lay toward the east. Beginning around 911 B.C.E., the political focus changed, and new political factors ushered in a predominantly north-south axis.[28] To the north Babylonia encountered Assyrian military strength again—this time due to the resurgence of Assyria under Ashur-dan II (934–912) and Adad-nirari II (911–891). In the south a new tribal group that would eventually become an important political player in Babylonian history first began to make its presence known: the Chaldeans. At the end of this period, Shamshi-Adad V of Assyria invaded Babylonia for four successive years (814–811). After the capture and deportation of two Babylonian kings to Assyria in 813 and 812, the country was reduced to a point of anarchy. One Babylonian chronicle reports that "there was no king in the land," and this state of affairs seems to have lasted at least twelve years.[29] For the next two centuries Chaldeans in southern Babylonia would compete with Assyria for control of northern Babylonia.

5.3. CULTURAL FEATURES OF THE EARLY NEO-BABYLONIAN PERIOD

The entire region experienced a gradual aramaization during these centuries, which only intensified during the middle centuries of the first millennium B.C.E. and persisted until the close of cuneiform culture. However, among the scribes of the early Neo-Babylonian period (and among the later Neo-Babylonian kings themselves, as we shall see) there persisted so great a devotion to the past and to the venerable Babylonian cultural traditions that the Akkadian language and its unwieldy cuneiform writing system endured. Even as Aramaic, with its obvious alphabetic advantages, gained momentum throughout the ancient world and eventually became the *lingua franca* under later Achaemenid rule, Akkadian language and literature continued in use. In fact, we have evidence of inscriptions composed in both Sumerian and Akkadian during this period and of prose embellished with poetic features, so that we may be assured of a burgeoning literature.[30] We may also presume an abundance of Aramaic texts were produced in Babylonia during the first millennium B.C.E. Unlike Babylonian, most of these Aramaic inscriptions were written on parchment or papyrus and have not survived. Our knowledge of Aramaic during this period is therefore limited mostly to notations on potsherds or on clay tablets.[31]

In general, early Neo-Babylonian culture and literature were continuations of developments during the Kassite period. Many of the great works of Babylonian literature and science that developed in the Old Babylonian and Kassite periods were standardized into a corpus, which has been called a "stream of tradition" not unlike a canonization process and which remained unchanged throughout most of the remainder of Babylonian history.[32] Certain early Babylonian poems survived only in second-millennium copies and were not collected in the libraries in the so-called "canon," although technically "scribal curriculum" is better.[33] Otherwise, much of what we may consider to be Babylonian belles-lettres was preserved in early Neo-Babylonian schools, carefully copied and transmitted during the early part of the first millennium, which was a time of intense interest in the past and, specifically, a time of commitment to preserving the great literary accomplishments of Babylonia's heritage. Along with the rise of the god of Babylon, Marduk, the rising influence of Marduk's son, Nabû (the god of writing), throughout Mesopotamia at this time (in both Assyria and Babylonia) was an important feature of cultural life and no doubt relates to the survival of literary and scientific traditions in the scribal community.[34]

One of the great accomplishments of ancient Mesopotamian literati is the Babylonian Epic of Creation, better known by the Akkadian title, *Enūma Eliš*.[35] Centered around the traditional mythological theme of theomachy (mighty combat among the deities), the *Enūma Eliš* relates primordial events in which Tiamat, the saltwater matrix deity, in collusion with her husband and eleven divine monsters of her own creation, threatens the other gods. The terrified deities persuade the champion-hero of the epic, Marduk, to represent them in combat with Tiamat, agreeing to concede to Marduk supremacy in the pantheon if he is successful against her.[36] At the central fourth tablet (of seven), the battle rages, and Marduk is successful. Using Tiamat's massive cadaver, the victorious Marduk creates the present universe, and using the blood of her husband and co-conspirator, Qingu, he creates humankind to do the hard labor of the universe, leaving the deities free from work. Finally, as a permanent memorial to Marduk's splendor, the city of Babylon is established as his luxurious resting place. The piece ends with the gods assembling for a feast at Esagil, Marduk's new temple, where they acknowledge him as supreme deity of the universe and close with an enumeration of his fifty honorific names. The list of Marduk's names, which comprises approximately one-fourth of the total composition, meticulously explains the etymological significance of each name and serves to illustrate the extent of Babylonian erudition.

None of our copies of the seven tablets of the *Enūma Eliš* antedates the first millennium B.C.E., and the date of composition is a debated issue. Although many have assumed the epic was composed during the Kassite period, a stronger case can be made for slightly later based on the epic's overarching purpose.[37] We routinely refer to it as a creation myth, yet in reality the central theme of the *Enūma Eliš* is not creation at all, but the exaltation of Marduk and justification of his supremacy at the head of the pantheon.[38] The epic thus reflects an era when the city of Babylon had risen politically and even replaced Nippur as the traditional locus of divine power in the world and a new sense of nationalism had emerged with Babylon at the center of a world empire.[39] The reign of Nebuchadnezzar I (especially the return of the statue of Marduk from Elam) spawned a flurry of literary activity celebrating the elevation of Marduk,[40] and it seems likely that this is when the epic was composed, although it no doubt relied on earlier hymnic-epic materials (see fig. 5.2).[41]

During later Babylonian history, the *Enūma Eliš* composition was quoted on the fourth day of the New Year festival at Babylon and played a significant role in the religious and social life of the community. Although the New Year festival (the so-called *akītū* festival) was celebrated at the city of Ur as early as the Neo-Sumerian period, the festival assumed new religious significance during the early Neo-Babylonian period.[42] The twelve days of the festival were celebrated at Babylon in Nisannu around the time of the vernal equinox. Previously, diverse ceremonies were performed at many different cities in Babylonia over a long period of time and for deities other than Marduk. However, during this period the festival ritual required collecting all the deities to Babylon and confirming the kingship of the gods to Marduk.[43] Besides marking the calendrical and agricultural significance of the Near Year, the ritual called for prayers to Marduk on behalf of the city of Babylon, a ritual cleansing of his temple, a symbolic enthronement of Marduk ("taking the hands of Bel"), as well as a symbolic recitation of the *Enūma Eliš* on the fourth day of the festival. The religious and symbolic significance of the festival in Babylonian culture of the first millennium is best illustrated by the way the Babylonian chronicles (see discussion in ch. 6 below) carefully note those times when the *akītū* festival was suspended due to political weakness.[44]

The rise of Marduk in the Babylonian pantheon, accompanied by the impressive *Enūma Eliš* and a new significance of the New Year festival, reflect significant religious developments during this period. It has recently been argued that the Babylonians became a people "of an almighty god" at this time, suggesting that they accepted Marduk not only as creator of the world but as personally stronger than all other powers combined, which occasionally led to ill-advised decisions, especially in

Fig. 5.2. Cuneiform tablet relating the Epic of Creation.
Dated to the seventh century B.C.E., this tablet was excavated at Nineveh.
© Copyright The British Museum.

regard to warfare.[45] The degree to which we can speak specifically about the nature of these theological convictions is questionable, and it is unlikely the ancient Babylonians would have stressed anything like exclusive absolute power for Marduk. After all, his son Nabû also rose in prominence during the same period or shortly afterward. However, it is helpful to hold these developments together as a general widespread "theology of exaltation" at work in the ancient world during the Iron Age, which involved both Israelite worshipers of Yhwh in the west and Babylonian worshipers of Marduk in the east.[46]

Finally, a word about our admittedly limited examples of visual art from the early Neo-Babylonian period, which nonetheless also reflects a retrospective attitude. Such examples of art as are, in fact, available to us are generally stifled, and artistry may be seen in decline, although most of our examples come only from *kudurru* stelae.[47] As in other features of early Neo-Babylonian culture, the art of the period tends to reflect a return to earlier classical forms.[48] This deep conservatism of early Neo-Babylonian culture must be stated with caution, however, because the massive building projects of later centuries left little evidence in Babylon and other urban centers, and we therefore lack archaeological specifics.[49]

6

THE NEO-BABYLONIAN PERIOD

Events in Mesopotamia during the first millennium B.C.E. were domi-
nated by a series of imperial powers, primarily the Assyrian Empire, the
Persian Empire, and, later, the arrival of Alexander the Great and Greek
rule. However, for a brief period during the seventh and sixth centuries,
Babylon rose again to premier international status and enjoyed a spectacular period of strength and prosperity. On the one hand, the
Neo-Babylonian Empire (also sometimes known, less appropriately, as the
Chaldean Empire) may be perceived as a mere interlude between the
Assyrians and Persians, a period of extremely brief duration. On the other
hand, the grandeur of the empire, especially under Nebuchadnezzar II, and
its legacy in the biblical and classical sources, left an indelible mark on
subsequent history, making this one of the most important and interesting
periods of ancient Babylonian history. This final chapter will cover the rise
and fall of the empire, beginning with the arrival of newcomers and their
role in a "new" Babylonia.

6.1. CHALDEANS, ARAMEANS, AND THE EMERGENCE OF A NEW BABYLONIA

The Chaldeans of southern Babylonia first appear in the cuneiform
sources of the ninth century B.C.E. They were more sedentary than the
Arameans, who continued to plague western Babylonia as loosely organized seminomads. The Chaldeans were organized in tribal groups called
"houses" and were settled in the swamps and lakes of the lower courses
of the Tigris and Euphrates Rivers. The largest and most influential
Chaldean tribes were Bit-Dakkuri south of Borsippa, Bit-Amukani further
south along the Euphrates, and Bit-Yakin to the east along the Tigris (see
fig. 6.1). The smaller Aramean tribes were loosely organized around the
fringes of the settled areas.[1] The Chaldeans and Arameans were both West
Semitic, and many in the past have assumed they were identical. However,
the native Assyrian and Babylonian sources consistently distinguished
between them. They are also distinguished by the differences in tribal
organization, the dates of their respective appearances in history, and the
contrasting levels of Babylonization.[2] Assyrian perceptions of Babylonia to

the south during this period provide fascinating insight into the political and ethnic realities of the day. The terms "Akkad" and "Akkadian" refer occasionally to the ancient city by that name but more frequently to northern Babylonia as opposed to the southern part (ancient Sumer), now inhabited by the tribal groups. Thus the old settled population of the land, which carried on the classical Babylonian culture, were "Akkadians," as distinct from the Chaldeans and Arameans.[3]

The Chaldeans seemed to have adapted quickly to Babylonian culture, controlling the trade routes of the Persian Gulf area and thereby accumulating considerable wealth with which they paid handsome tribute to the Assyrians. But this was only a temporary ploy, since all the while they were growing in number and strength. Chaldeans became contenders for the Babylonian throne by the middle of the eighth century. Indeed, the first quarter of the millennium can be described as a time of gradual transition from Kassite to Chaldean dominance, impeded by Aramean incursions and, eventually, Assyrian interference in Babylonian independence.[4]

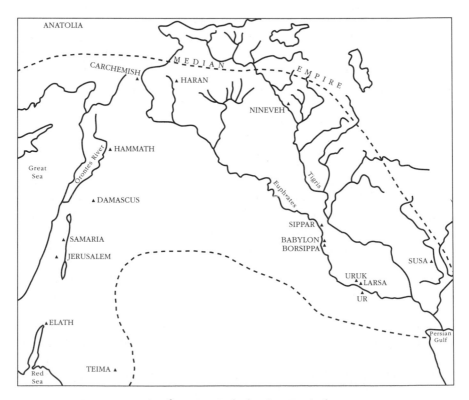

Fig. 6.1. Neo-Babylonian Period.

Conflict between Assyria and Babylonia during the ninth century had weakened northern Babylonia considerably. With the death of Adad-nirari III (783), the Assyrian Empire was also temporarily halted by weak central government, economic problems and a new threat to its north, Urartu.[5] The Chaldeans were now ready to fill the political vacuum created by a declining Assyria and a ravaged northern Babylonia. Although details are at present sketchy due to a severe lack of documentary evidence, it appears that the first powerful Chaldean monarch was a certain Eriba-Marduk from the Bit-Yakin tribe. Later tradition honors him with the title "re-establisher of the foundation(s) of the land," which presumably means he restored the stability of Babylonia. Evidence is insufficient to determine his dates precisely, but he reigned for at least nine years, and his rule terminated shortly before 760 B.C.E. He drove out the Arameans, who had inhabited portions of Babylon and Borsippa, repaired the throne of Marduk at Esagil, and engaged in other building activities.[6]

The next noteworthy ruler of Babylon marked the beginning of a new era for later historians. From the time of Nabonassar (747–734 B.C.E.), ancient scholars began to keep systematically precise records of historical events. The Neo-Babylonian Chronicle series, a valuable new historiographic source for this period, records outstanding events of each year beginning with the reign of Nabonassar.[7] Greek astronomers recognized the "Nabonassar era" as a turning point in the history of science, and the term "Chaldean" came to mean "astronomer" in Hellenistic times.[8]

Nabonassar was evidently not Chaldean, and he apparently attempted to exclude Chaldeans from power. His inability to control either the Chaldeans or Arameans left Babylonia hemmed in on every hand, and he was able to maintain order only with the help of a new neighbor to the north. Tiglath-Pileser III rose to the throne of Assyria as the result of a revolution (745 B.C.E.) and quickly established his reputation as an empire builder. He sustained Nabonassar's reign, and Babylonia appears to have stabilized economically during his reign, as evidenced by the number of economic texts available.[9] Soon after Nabonassar's death, however, Babylonia was weakened by minor revolts.

Mukin-zeri (also known as Nabu-mukin-zeri), a Chaldean from southern Babylonia, took advantage of the instability in Babylon and assumed the throne in 731. He was from the Bit-Amukani tribe of the Chaldeans, but little else is known of him.[10] Tiglath-Pileser had been preoccupied in Syria but moved to depose Mukin-zeri, which he finally accomplished three years later. In an attempt to consolidate his hold on the south, Tiglath-Pileser himself assumed the throne of Babylon. He thus became the first Assyrian ruler in more than four centuries to unite Assyria and Babylonia in a dual monarchy, setting a precedent for Assyrian rulers for the next century.[11]

Tiglath-Pileser's son, Shalmaneser V (726–722), inherited the dual monarchy and successfully ruled Babylon for five years. Soon after his death, another Chaldean, Merodach-baladan II, seized the Babylonian throne and consolidated his hold by uniting the previously fragmented Chaldean tribes. A wealthy prince of the Bit-Yakin tribe, Merodach-baladan was also able to secure a military alliance with Elam to the east in his anti-Assyrian efforts. The Hebrew Bible also bears testimony to his capable diplomatic efforts at forging an international coalition against Assyria (2 Kgs 20:12–19; Isa 39).[12] This consummate politician and military strategist was able to rule Babylonia—free from Assyrian interference—for a full decade (721–710). The evidence suggests that Chaldean rule was not univocally accepted throughout Babylonia, but Merodach-baladan managed to placate, or at least dominate, the small pro-Assyrian faction in the urban centers of northern Babylonia, while staying one step ahead of the Assyrians by avoiding direct contact with their overwhelming military forces.[13]

Ultimately, however, Sargon II (721–705) and the might of the Neo-Assyrian Empire proved too much. In 710 Sargon ousted Merodach-baladan and assumed the throne of Babylonia in a dual monarchy for five years. Nevertheless, Merodach-baladan's brief reign illustrates the recurring movement in Babylonia to retain national autonomy free of Assyrian rule. The unity and spirit of independence that he established among the Chaldean tribes of southern Babylonia culminated in the rise of the Neo-Babylonian Empire, which eventually would participate in the destruction of Assyria.

For the century after Merodach-baladan, the powerful monarchs of the Neo-Assyrian Empire expended considerable energy and resources trying to maintain control of Babylonia. Sargon's son and successor, Sennacherib (704–681), tried several modes of governing Babylonia.[14] First he himself assumed the throne of the dual monarchy as his predecessors had done. Successive revolts one month apart led Sennacherib to try a new strategy, installing a pro-Assyrian native Babylonian. After this too failed, Sennacherib finally installed his son, the crown prince, on the throne of Babylon. But the young prince was captured and taken to Elam, where he was presumably murdered. After a decade and a half of trouble in the south and the loss of his son, Sennacherib ruthlessly devastated Babylon. For the next eight years until his death, the city languished with no official king, although there is evidence that southern Babylonia suffered less economically than did the north.[15]

Esarhaddon (680–669) abandoned his father's austere anti-Babylonian attitude and resumed control of Babylonia under the dual monarchy of previous Assyrian monarchs. During his reign, enforced Assyrian rule provided stability in Babylonia, and the country appears to have experienced gradual economic growth and moderate prosperity.[16] Upon

Esarhaddon's death, the empire was divided according to his instructions between his sons: Ashurbanipal (668–627) was king in Assyria, and Shamash-shum-ukin (667–648) ruled in Babylonia. This arrangement was intended to perpetuate the peace and stability that Esarhaddon had provided, but this was not to be. The sibling kingdoms fell into a bloody civil war, and after four years (652–648) the Assyrians were able to regain control of the south. It seems likely that Manasseh of Judah joined Elam, Arabia, and various other anti-Assyrian forces in western Asia in a Babylonian coalition in support of Shamash-shum-ukin (which may be suggested by 2 Chr 33:11–13).[17]

Assyria emerged from the conflict seriously weaker; it had cost Ashurbanipal an inordinate amount of resources and energy to defeat Babylonia, and the vulnerability of the Assyrian Empire had become apparent. Moreover, Babylonia experienced a quick economic recovery from the war. The Assyrian threat to Babylonian nationalism actually served as a catalyst to unify resistance movements among the various tribal and ethnically diverse elements of Babylonia, which may explain the rapid rise and remarkable strength of the Neo-Babylonian Empire in light of the chaotic weakness of Babylonia in the early first millennium.[18] After the quick postwar economic and cultural recovery, Babylonia was on the threshold of political achievements comparable to Hammurapi's great empire over a millennium before.

6.2. NABOPOLASSAR AND NEBUCHADNEZZAR: INNOVATIONS AND LEGACY

With the death of Ashurbanipal, Nabopolassar (625–605 B.C.E.) seized the throne of Babylon and established a new dynasty variously known as the Neo-Babylonian or Chaldean Empire. However, the use of "Chaldean" as a designation for this period may be misleading. The term is used by biblical and classical authors to denote this dynasty, but in these sources "Chaldean" is usually synonymous for "Babylonian" and has no ethnic significance. There is no unambiguous evidence that Nabopolassar and his successors were ethnically Chaldean.[19]

Early in Nabopolassar's reign, the Assyrian military machine was still very much a threat to Babylonian independence. Several royal inscriptions from his reign, mostly in the form of barrel-shaped clay cylinders,[20] credit Nabopolassar with either destroying the Assyrian forces altogether, or at least driving them from Babylonian soil.[21] Interestingly, Nabopolassar's royal inscriptions do not project an image of Babylonian imperialism, nor do they make any self-conscious claims that he, Nabopolassar, is heir to the Assyrian Empire. Rather, it appears his reign was preoccupied with driving the Assyrian army from Babylonia, and subsequently Nabopolassar remained focused on consolidating local rule.[22] These features of the

Neo-Babylonian royal inscriptions would change dramatically under Nebuchadnezzar, as we shall see.

Whatever the extent of Nabopolassar's military successes against the Assyrians, he managed to hold power with only brief interludes until 614, when a new power in ancient Near Eastern politics laid siege to Ashur, one of the four great capitals of Assyria. The newcomers, the Medes, were successors to Elamite power in Iran, and under Cyaxares (625–585) they took the city of Ashur and began massacring its inhabitants.[23] Nabopolassar arrived on the scene after the city had actually fallen, and by the ruins of Ashur he established an alliance with his new powerful neighbor, Cyaxares.[24] This treaty delegated northern Mesopotamia to the Medes and left Nabopolassar free in central Mesopotamia and Syria. He was a major participant in the fall of the other Assyrian capitals, including Nineveh, an event reflected in biblical prophetic traditions (Nahum; Zeph 2:13–15).

Assyria's last gasp was a futile alliance with Egypt, who, in a sudden reversal of policy, realized Babylonia was now its main threat. In 609 Josiah, king of Judah, attempted to block the path of Pharaoh Neco II at Megiddo, who was headed north to assist the remnants of the Assyrian army near Carchemish on the northwest bend of the Euphrates. Although Josiah lost his life in the attempt (2 Kgs 23:29; 2 Chr 35:20–23), his involvement impaired the Egyptians and contributed to the Babylonian victory. Because of old age or ill health, Nabopolassar began leaving the command of the Babylonian army to the crown prince, Nebuchadnezzar II (605–562).[25] Early in Nabopolassar's reign he had designated his son as "chief son, the crown prince," which was necessary because there was no principle of dynastic succession in Babylonia.[26] The young general led his forces in an impressive and decisive victory against the Egyptians at Carchemish in the spring of 605 B.C.E. (Jer 46:2). All of Syria-Palestine lay before Nebuchadnezzar as he pursued the Egyptians south. But in mid-August Nabopolassar died in Babylon, and Nebuchadnezzar raced across the desert and claimed the throne in less than a month.[27] In December of 604 Nebuchadnezzar's forces captured the city of Ashkelon and took its king prisoner.[28] These events no doubt caused great anxiety in neighboring Jerusalem (2 Kgs 24:1, 7), and they can in fact be synchronized with a sacred fast "before the LORD," in which inhabitants of the towns of Judah came to Jerusalem (Jer 36:9).

Nebuchadnezzar quickly fell heir to most of the former territories of the Assyrian Empire. It used to be routinely assumed that there was an easy transference of power "from Nineveh to Babylon" and that Babylonian imperial geography divided into provincial units along similar lines as the Assyrian Empire.[29] However, at present we have no Neo-Babylonian administrative or royal inscriptions that detail how the provinces were administered, and the evidence for such a structured Neo-Babylonian provincial system is incomplete. The royal inscriptions available to us evince a rhetoric and ideology notably in contrast to their Assyrian predecessors (see below), and it is possible that this contrast corresponds to a difference in attitudes of imperial administration of the western provinces.[30] Others have countered that the evidence currently available should not lead us to assume a decided break administratively between the Assyrian Empire and that of Nebuchadnezzar.[31] For the meantime, it seems likely that we will be unable to make out the specifics of such a system because of the brevity of the Babylonian dynasty and because of significant gaps in the documentation.

With the friendly Medes consolidating their power to the north and east, Nebuchadnezzar was free to concentrate on the Euphrates Valley and Syria-Palestine as far as Egypt. Thus he was able once again to establish Babylonia as the leading power in the ancient Near East, and his reign may be compared to Hammurapi's in strength and size. There were, however, pockets of resistance, especially in Palestine. Moreover, Nebuchadnezzar unwisely marched against Egypt in 601. The site of the actual battle is not known, but both sides suffered great losses, and Nebuchadnezzar was forced to withdraw without having actually reached Egypt itself.[32] Assuming that Egypt was now the stronger of the two world powers, Jehoiakim of Judah suddenly switched allegiance away from Babylonia.[33] Nebuchadnezzar personally led the Babylonian forces to Judah. Jehoiakim died before the siege of Jerusalem, leaving his son Jehoiachin on the throne. The exact date of Jerusalem's fall is recorded in the Babylonian Chronicle (16 March 597 B.C.E.), which reflects the strategic importance the city held at this time (see fig. 6.2).[34] Nebuchadnezzar captured Jehoiachin, deported him and other members of the royal family to Babylon, and replaced him with an uncle, Zedekiah (2 Kgs 24:17).

In 595, Nebuchadnezzar faced an insurrection attempt in Babylon.[35] Zedekiah, who oscillated between a begrudging loyalty to Babylonia and open rebellion, took the opportunity to lead Judah in aligning itself once again with Egypt. Against the advice of pro-Babylonian voices in Judah, especially the haunting voice of Jeremiah, of course, Zedekiah hosted a conference in Jerusalem for representatives from Tyre, Sidon, Edom, Moab, and Ammon, for the purpose of plotting rebellion against Babylon (Jer 27:1–11). However, Nebuchadnezzar easily suppressed the insurrection at home within a few months and promptly returned to Syria-Palestine to accept the tribute of its rulers,[36] presumably squelching any notion of rebellion in the west for the meantime.

Ultimately, however, Zedekiah and other leaders in Syria-Palestine continued to believe that Babylonia's presence in the west was tenuous. The long history of Egypt's dominance of the region, combined with Nebuchadnezzar's inability to humble Egypt in 601, fed the flames of independence and created hope for those who wanted to throw off the Babylonian yoke. Thus when a new pharaoh, Psammetichus II, led Egypt to a convincing victory against Nubia in 591 B.C.E., and followed this with an apparent victory parade into Syria-Palestine publicizing his Nubian

Fig. 6.2. Portion of the Babylonian Chronicle recording the capture of Jerusalem in 597 B.C.E.
© Copyright The British Museum.

successes, all anti-Babylonian sentiments would have been greatly encouraged.[37] Unfortunately, the Babylonian Chronicles for Nebuchadnezzar are broken after his eleventh year (594/593 B.C.E.), and therefore the precise date for Zedekiah's final rebellion is unknown (2 Kgs 24:20). It seems likely, however, that he was encouraged by renewed Egyptian presence in the region.

Most likely Psammetichus had intended to lead all of Syria-Palestine into rebellion against the Babylonians. But Nebuchadnezzar's strength and resolve were greatly misjudged. He laid siege to Jerusalem on 15 January 587 (2 Kgs 25:1; Jer 39:1; Ezek 24:1–2), and it fell on 19 July 586 (2 Kgs 25:3). Without the benefit of the Babylonian Chronicle series at this point, these dates are somewhat in question, perhaps off by as much as one year; that is, the siege may have begun in January 588, and the fall of the city therefore took place in July 587.[38] Regardless of the chronological specifics, letters from the nearby city of Lachish bear eloquent testimony to conditions during the eighteen-month siege. One of these letters states, "we are watching the (fire)-signals of Lachish ... because we cannot see Azekah."[39] Azekah, which was between Jerusalem and Lachish and was presumably supposed to relay messages by smoke signal, had apparently already fallen to the Babylonians.[40] The book of Jeremiah confirms that Lachish and Azekah were the best-defended cities in Judah; apart from Jerusalem itself, these two were the last fortified cities of the kingdom to fall (Jer 34:6–7). Zedekiah's trust in the Egyptians was a disastrous miscalculation. Psammetichus himself fell ill and died while Jerusalem was under siege, and Zedekiah's appeal for help from the new pharaoh, Apries, resulted in a small Egyptian force nearly a year after the siege had begun (Jer 37:5; Ezek 17:15–17; see also Josephus, *Ant.* 10.108–110). It was little more than a diversion for the Babylonians.

Jerusalem finally succumbed to hunger, and the Babylonians breached the wall in July 586 B.C.E. (2 Kgs 25:3–4). Zedekiah at first escaped but was subsequently captured, tortured, and dragged off to Babylon (2 Kgs 25:4–7). Beginning 16 August 586, at Nebuchadnezzar's directive to his general, Nebuzaradan, the city and the temple were thoroughly razed (2 Kgs 25:8–9). The trauma of this event left an indelible and unmistakable imprint on the postexilic Jews. Indeed, it has been argued that the entire macrostructure of the Hebrew Scriptures revolves around the narration of this event as its apex; thus, the loss of city, temple, and monarchy is the conclusion of the Primary History and the center point of the Latter Prophets and the Writings.[41] In addition to the loss of these central institutions and its impact on Israel's Scriptures, the Babylonian deportations of the Judean population in 597, 586, 582, and perhaps others, established the distinction between homeland and Diaspora, which is a lasting feature of Judaism and Jewish life.

Archaeological evidence confirms the extent of the destruction, resulting in a virtual vacuum culturally for the so-called Babylonian period of Syro-Palestinian history (605–539 B.C.E.). Although perhaps an overstatement of the facts, it has been argued recently that such towns and villages as existed during this period were very poorly populated, and all were poorly functioning.[42] Although estimates of population size for cities and regions of antiquity are fraught with problems of inadequate data and methodological uncertainties, recent surface surveys of Judah and Benjamin nevertheless suggest that the population of Yehud was approximately 13,350 during the early Persian period (the late-sixth/early-fifth centuries B.C.E.) and approximately 20,650 for the later Persian period (late-fifth/early-fourth centuries B.C.E.). Jerusalem itself averaged approximately 1,500 citizens during this time, which has been approximated as 20 percent of its size prior to its destruction by Nebuchadnezzar.[43] The degree of devastation wrought by the Babylonians may be illustrated further by contrasting these figures with the eighth-century population of Judah, estimated at 110,000.[44] Judah apparently attempted independence once more in 582, but this was easily squelched by Nebuzaradan (Jer 52:30).

The scope of Nebuchadnezzar's imperial aspirations may be seen in his thirteen-year siege and apparent victory at Tyre (Josephus, *Ag. Ap.* 1:21; Ezek 26:7–14) and his invasion of Egypt in 570 B.C.E. However, it should be noted that historical evidence from the latter part of Nebuchadnezzar's reign is sparse and that the evidence of his Egyptian invasion is open to other interpretations.[45] Nonetheless, his empire surpassed Hammurapi's in geographical dimensions, and his inscriptions reflect a royal ideology different from those of his father, Nabopolassar (see map on p. 88). A new Babylonian imperialism emerged in which hegemony became the means by which the king could fulfill his obligation to rebuild, refurbish, and supply Babylonia's cult centers, the king became the protector of all humanity; and the city of Babylon became the economic and administrative center of the world.[46] In his inscriptional remains Nebuchadnezzar prided himself first and foremost in domestic rebuilding activities.[47] Indeed, his military campaigns were motivated to a large degree by the desire to take war spoils to finance his ambitious rebuilding of Babylon and twelve other cities in Babylonia. While Nabopolassar's reign may be said to represent Babylonia in its phase of territorial liberation, Nebuchadnezzar's inscriptions record Babylonia's expansionist nationalism more generally.[48]

Nebuchadnezzar's legendary pride (Dan 4:30 [Heb. 4:27]) was not without justification. He was clearly responsible for transforming Babylon into the greatest city of the ancient world; its modern ruins spread over two thousand acres to form the largest ancient site in Mesopotamia.[49] Its magnificent walls were entered by eight gates, each named after a god. The famed Ishtar Gate played an important religious role in the life of the city and is fortunately the best preserved. The surface of the entrance was covered with blue enameled bricks, which served as background for alternating red-and-white dragons (symbolic of Marduk) and bulls (symbolic of Adad). The gate was approached by means of an impressive processional street, sixty-five feet wide in places and paved with white limestone and red breccia. Bordering the street were walls that were found still standing as high as forty feet. They were decorated with lions six feet in length (symbolic of Ishtar) with red or yellow manes on a blue ceramic background. It was along this street that the king would accompany the statue of Marduk in grand procession each spring during the New Year festival.[50] It was believed he and the inhabitants of Babylonia participated in the renewal of nature and the naming of destiny for the coming year.[51] One can only image the awe inspired by this ceremony in such a dazzling setting.

The Babylonian renaissance under Nabopolassar and Nebuchadnezzar brought with it a religious revitalization, which is reflected in a number of ways. In one particular propaganda document, Nebuchadnezzar is the "king of justice," the defender and protector of the innocent, the wise judge similar to Hammurapi before him, and one who is ardent in his devotion to Marduk.[52] The vitality of this period is also reflected in architecture. Perhaps the most famous structure is the seven-staged brick temple-tower named *Etemenanki* ("house of the foundation of heaven and earth"). The typical Mesopotamian pyramid (or *zigguratu,* "temple-tower") was a stepped pyramid that characterized virtually every major city from the late third millennium onward and that provided a physical focal point for a city, symbolizing its power and that of its god. Often the deity's temple was built on top of the tower.[53] In the Neo-Assyrian period, Sennacherib had destroyed the "tower of Babel," but it was repaired by both Nabopolassar and Nebuchadnezzar and must have been an imposing structure, with estimates of its height reaching three hundred feet.

There were a number of royal palaces, but Nebuchadnezzar built a magnificent new palace late in his reign. The ruins of this structure contained a museum in which he housed a large collection of "antiquities," revealing his interest in archaeology and history. Indeed scribes of his reign were particularly fascinated with Hammurapi's Old Babylonian kingdom, which they saw as a model for Nebuchadnezzar's own royal ideology. While they appear to have avoided Assyrian ideas of empire, they intentionally chose to apply Old Babylonian concepts and language, even mimicking the old lapidary script, resuscitating linguistic archaisms and archaizing orthographies, and frequently copying Old Babylonian inscriptions.[54]

As many as five classical writers described the famous Hanging Gardens of Babylon, including Berossus, who credited Nebuchadnezzar with building them.

> After he had walled the city in notable fashion and adorned its gates in a manner befitting a holy place, he built another palace next to the palace of his father [Nabopolassar]. . . . In this palace he built and arranged the so-called hanging garden by setting up high stone terraces which he made appear very similar to mountains planted with all kinds of trees. He did this because his wife who had been raised in Media longed for mountainous surroundings.[55]

Lack of references in the native Babylonian sources and in Herodotus has led some to doubt the very existence of the gardens, but parallels with such gardens built by Assyrian kings earlier and hints in Nebuchadnezzar's inscriptions at an elevated, stepped terrace of bricks located between the river canals and his northern palace make the existence of the gardens seem likely.[56] If so, then in addition to its many beautiful buildings and structures, including as many as fifty temples, the city of Babylon contained two of the Seven Wonders of the ancient world: the Hanging Gardens and the city walls.[57] A well-attested Babylonian document, the Topography of Babylon, which is essentially a scholarly compendium glorifying the city as a religious center, lists ten quarters of the city, each with its own temples and landmarks. Following a layout of the city as old as the thirteenth century B.C.E., Nebuchadnezzar built a remarkable city, which is coming to greater light thanks to a coordination of textual and archaeological data (see fig. 6.3).[58] Nebuchadnezzar II, then, was heir to the twelfth-century Nebuchadnezzar I (see ch. 5 above) not only in namesake but in royal epithets and in the ideology of Babylon as crystallized in the Topography of Babylon. Each exhibited the sense of national pride so common after political vindication and liberation.

While Babylonia enjoyed this remarkable revitalization under Nebuchadnezzar, cultural advances were being made also in Greece and Israel, in what some historians have considered the height of human civilization.[59] In Babylonia, Nebuchadnezzar died in the fall of 562 B.C.E. after a forty-three-year rule.[60] The royal titulary of his inscriptions contain allusions to him as a second Hammurapi, and scribes in his employ show a decided dependence on the laws of Hammurapi.[61] His reign is one of the most amply documented periods of Babylonian history, yielding royal inscriptions, chronicles, private and administrative texts, legal materials, and letters. It has recently been acknowledged that we now know more about the historical Nebuchadnezzar from primary sources than we do about Alexander the Great.[62] History has honored his dynasty as the apex of Babylonia's wealth and political power—but it would all be lost in less than a quarter of a century.

6.3. NEBUCHADNEZZAR'S SUCCESSORS

Nebuchadnezzar was followed in rapid succession by three ineffective dynasts: his son Amēl-Marduk (561–560), his son-in-law Neriglissar (559–556), and the latter's son Labashi-Marduk (556; see fig. 6.4).

Amēl-Marduk (Evil-Merodach in the biblical record) immediately released Jehoiachin, who had been imprisoned by Nebuchadnezzar for thirty-six years, and gave him royal recognition, including a regular allowance for the rest of his life (2 Kgs 25:27–30; Jer 52:31–34). Babylonian ration tablets from Nebuchadnezzar's reign shed light on Jehoiachin's imprisonment during his exile. These tablets, ranging in date from the tenth to the thirty-fifth year of Nebuchadnezzar (594–569 B.C.E.), list deliveries of oil for prisoners of war under house arrest, from Judea, Philistia, Phoenicia, and as far away as Egypt and Greece. Among several Judeans identified as foreigners in the texts, they include monthly rations of oil for *Ya'u-kīnu* (alternatively *Yakū-kīnu*), "king of the land of *Yaḫudu*" (or Judah).[63] Since Jehoiachin is referred to in these documents as "king of Judah," it is possible that during the long years of Nebuchadnezzar's reign the Babylonians were reserving the possibility of reinstating Jehoiachin in Jerusalem should they become dissatisfied with Zedekiah.[64] Amēl-Marduk's release of Jehoiachin may have occurred on the occasion of his enthronement, or perhaps as part of the New Year's festival in Babylon during his first year. It seems likely that Amēl-Marduk planned to reinstate Jehoiachin in Jerusalem as vassal. But the Babylonian king himself was dead the next year, and Jehoiachin died in exile.

Building inscriptions during the brief reign of Amēl-Marduk reveal a continued devotion to Marduk but limited repair work in Babylon. The king was evidently limited to internal affairs, since there appear to have been no military operations during his reign.[65]

The name of the next king, Neriglissar, has come down to us through classical sources (see Berossus below); he is Nergal-shar-uṣur in Babylonian sources and Nergal-sharezer in the Bible (Jer 39:3, 13). He had become a prominent businessman early in Nebuchadnezzar's reign and eventually became a high military official (*rab mugi, CAD* M/2, 171) during Nebuchadnezzar's western campaigns.[66] When the Babylonian economy began to suffer during the years of Amēl-Marduk's reign, Neriglissar consolidated his acquisition of land through various banking ventures.[67] His political influence and position may be noted also by his marriage to Kashaya, Nebuchadnezzar's daughter.

Neriglissar apparently assassinated Amēl-Marduk and took the throne himself.[68] His building inscriptions mention repairing the royal palace and the east bank of the Araḫtum canal, as well as continued work on Esagil, Marduk's temple in Babylon.[69] A chronicle from Neriglissar's third year (557) records a successful military campaign in Cilicia against a king who had raided a Babylonian protectorate in Syria.[70] Of Labashi-Marduk, little is known. The Uruk King List assigns him a reign of only three months, which is confirmed by the available economic texts dated to his reign.[71]

Nabonidus (556–539) was a usurper with no hereditary claim to the throne; that is, he was not from the royal family and could claim no support for the throne.[72] He was a leading figure in the murder of Nebuchadnezzar's grandson Labashi-Marduk, being part of a disenchanted faction blocked by the dynastic succession of Amēl-Marduk. Nabonidus's mother was Adad-guppi, a prominent centenarian from Haran, the important religious center in northern Mesopotamia. Her biography has been preserved on a tomb inscription that relates her remarkable devotion to

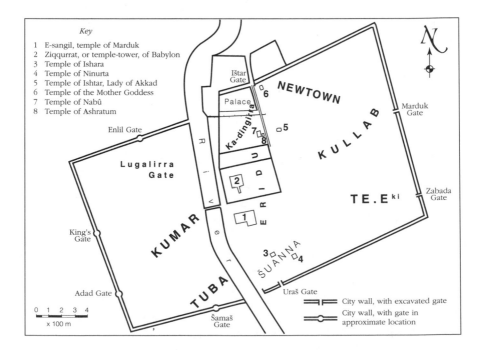

Fig. 6.3. Sketch map of Babylon.
Courtesy of Andrew George, "Babylon Revisited:
Archaeology and Philology in Harness," *Antiquity* 67 (1993): 739.

Sîn, the moon god of Haran.[73] This may explain Nabonidus's rabid devotion to Sîn, while paying lip service to other deities of Babylonia.

Nabonidus participated in the conspiracy against Labashi-Marduk, although he apparently never intended kingship for himself. He would have already been considerably advanced in age at the time of his accession, since his mother, Adad-guppi, died at 102 years of age in his ninth

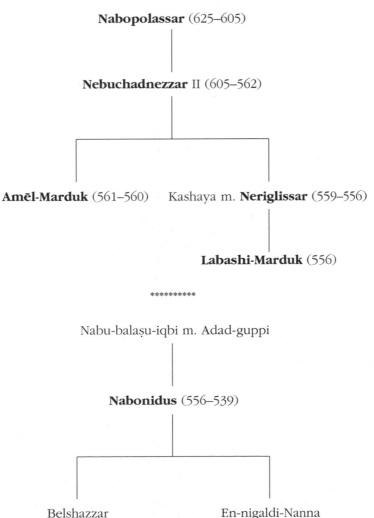

Nabopolassar (625–605)

Nebuchadnezzar II (605–562)

Amēl-Marduk (561–560)   Kashaya m. **Neriglissar** (559–556)

Labashi-Marduk (556)

****

Nabu-balaṣu-iqbi m. Adad-guppi

Nabonidus (556–539)

Belshazzar   En-nigaldi-Nanna
                    high priestess of Ur

Fig. 6.4. Neo-Babylonian Kings.

regnal year.[74] It is probable that the conspirators were led by Belshazzar, Nabonidus's son. As the safest way to secure the throne for himself in the future, Belshazzar championed his father as the new ruler, while he himself may have been the real power behind the throne throughout Nabonidus's reign.[75] Nabonidus appears at times to be a man haunted by his conscience and uncertain of his own legitimacy to the throne. His staunch devotion to Sîn proved particularly unpopular to the Babylonian citizenry. His antiquarian interests surpassed those of his predecessors, and they were probably motivated by a political design to show continuity with the great Sargonic empire of the late third millennium.[76] Such enthusiasm for the past led Nabonidus to become something of an archaeologist, boasting that he had uncovered inscriptions of Hammurapi at Larsa and of Sargon I and Naram-Sin at Akkad. Also typical of this period are royal bricks and cylinders inscribed in a script mimicking Old Babylonian styles.

In 1986 Iraqi archaeologists from the University of Baghdad were excavating the Ebabbar temple of Shamash at Sippar and discovered a Neo-Babylonian library of as many as two thousand tablets, most of which were literary in nature.[77] It is believed that the library was found in a portion of the temple built by Nabonidus. Many of these texts were described in their colophons as "copied from originals" from Babylon, Nippur, Akkad, and so forth. Some of them were copies on clay of inscriptions originally written on stone stelae, and some were Neo-Babylonian copies of texts up to fifteen hundred years older. Whether or not the library was commissioned and preserved by Nabonidus himself, the discovery of this collection illustrates vividly the intense interest of Neo-Babylonian rulers and scholars in the past. As scholars have opportunity to study these texts further, they may richly supplement the documentary sources from the period. We have abundant documentation of Babylonian social and economic life, especially from the archives of the temple of Eanna, the shrine of Ishtar in Uruk, and that of the temple of Shamash in Sippar.[78] But more royal inscriptions, and especially more documents from the central administration, such as exist in abundance for the Neo-Assyrian Empire, would be especially welcome.

In the first year of his reign Nabonidus traveled to southern Babylonia bearing gold, silver, and precious stones, apparently in an attempt to legitimize his reign and galvanize his support.[79] Besides the royal inscriptions, we have economic texts from Larsa and Uruk demonstrating that Nabonidus himself was personally involved in the administration of the Eanna temple in Uruk and in requiring provisions be made for the temple, just as they had been done earlier during the time of Nebuchadnezzar II.[80]

For reasons that are still unclear, Nabonidus installed Belshazzar as regent in Babylon three years after he became king, and he then led an army through Syria, Lebanon, and finally into northwestern Arabia. He stayed ten years at the Arabian oasis of Teima (biblical Tema), five hundred miles from Babylonia, failing to return to the capital for the annual New Year festival honoring Marduk. It seems likely that Belshazzar and his supporters convinced Nabonidus to go into voluntary exile in Arabia, hoping to avoid confrontation between Nabonidus's religious convictions (on which, more below) and the powerful clergy of Marduk at Babylon. His banishment to Teima is thus explained as the result of political differences between Nabonidus and his powerful son.[81] On the other hand, it is possible he simply used Teima as a military outpost from which he commandeered the Arabian caravan routes and secured the surrender of other rich oases.[82] Whatever his personal motivation, his subjects in Babylon considered Nabonidus's prolonged absence a self-imposed exile.[83] The Persian captors of the city of Babylon in October 539 claimed they were liberating the city from a negligent ruler who was hated by his subjects.[84]

For over seventy years it has been commonly assumed that the stories of Nebuchadnezzar in the biblical book of Daniel, and especially his dementia recorded in Dan 4, are a conflation of traditions and legends related to the reign of Nabonidus instead. The discovery of an Aramaic text among scrolls from the Judean Desert (commonly, the "Dead Sea Scrolls"), known as the *Prayer of Nabonidus,* contains striking parallels with Dan 4 and specifically names Nabonidus.[85] Others have garnered numerous objections to these parallels and have maintained instead that the events of Nebuchadnezzar's life are actually closer to the stories of Dan 1–6 than the details of Nabonidus's reign.[86] There can be no doubt that many of the Daniel stories circulated in a kind of cycle of folklore and that our present book of Daniel preserves some of these traditions.[87] It has recently been argued that the redactor of the book of Daniel did in fact have a correct knowledge of history in the postexilic period and that he intentionally chose to represent the character of Nebuchadnezzar as he thought he *should be represented* for purposes of the book's message. In doing so, he relied freely on materials associated with Nabonidus because they conveniently contributed to the description of Nebuchadnezzar that the author desired in the narrative. The result was a paradigmatic description of the rebellious and boastful monarch, a warning for any future monarch who dared to mimic or repeat the blasphemous mistakes of the one who destroyed Jerusalem.[88]

The most remarkable features of Nabonidus are two innovations, which may fairly be said to characterize his reign. First, Nabonidus endeavored to elevate Sîn, the moon god, to chief position in the pantheon, consequently demoting Marduk of Babylon, who had been patron deity of the Babylonian state since at least the time of Nebuchadnezzar I in the Early Neo-Babylonian period (see ch. 5 above).[89] His royal inscriptions reflect a theological shift at about the time he returned from his ten-year residency at Teima. Prior to this time, in conformity to Neo-Babylonian predecessors, his royal inscriptions acknowledge Marduk as the god who made him king and as the one who established divine authority for his imperial rule. After this time, however, Sîn assumes this role in Nabonidus's texts.[90] This nonconformist ideological theme in the royal inscriptions of Nabonidus has long been the topic of scholarly investigation, but recently several have warned that the evidence has been misinterpreted.[91] It must be admitted that much of our evidence comes from Haran, where one might expect expressions of devotion to Sîn, and that other evidence comes from the Persian victors of Babylonia, whose claims to be liberators from an unpopular religious reformer were propagandistic. However, the chronological sequence of Nabonidus's devotion to Sîn vis-à-vis Marduk is persuasive, and at present I find the interpretation of Nabonidus as a religious reformer explains the evidence satisfactorily, although care should be taken not to overstate the case.

The second innovation of Nabonidus was an attempt to alter the imperial ideology so carefully shaped by Nabopolassar, and especially Nebuchadnezzar II. Breaking from their example, Nabonidus attempted to establish continuity between his own reign and that of the Sargonid kings of Assyria.[92] In both form and content, Nabonidus modified literary patterns used by his Neo-Babylonian predecessors in an attempt to portray himself as the legitimate successor to Ashurbanipal, especially. By contrast, the inscriptions of Nebuchadnezzar II echoed Old Babylonian concepts and language, and he and his scribes clearly viewed Hammurapi's era as a model for a new Babylonian imperialism, apparently taking great care to *avoid* dependence on Assyrian ideology. In a distinct departure from this ideology, Nabonidus's inscriptions appear to revive Assyrian conceptions of imperialism.[93]

A fascinating perception of this period from a later time is acquired by means of the so-called Uruk Prophecy, a "predicting" present-future prophecy, in which an author presents a historical event as though it were still in the future for propagandistic purposes. The most likely interpretation of this damaged tablet is that it "predicts" (through *vaticinium ex eventu,* or prophecy after the fact) the rise of Nabopolassar, the world-wide dominion of Nebuchadnezzar, and the everlasting reign of the Neo-Babylonian dynasty.[94] The historical context of the prophecy may have been literati who composed materials in support of the rule of Nebuchadnezzar II and Amēl-Marduk and in condemnation of their successors, especially Neriglissar, who did not fulfill the expectations of the Uruk establishment. This material was later recast in the Uruk Prophecy, whose purpose was to show to a Seleucid ruler of the first half of the third century the proper royal conduct toward the city.[95]

In October 539 B.C.E., the city of Babylon fell to Cyrus, an event attested in native Babylonian and Persian sources, as well as Hellenistic sources (Herodotus, 1.178, 190–291; Xenophon, *Cyropaedia* 7.5.26–30) and the Bible (Dan 5:30).[96] The Persian capture of Babylon ended the last native Semitic empire in ancient Mesopotamia, and therefore Nabonidus and his coregent, Belshazzar, were the last native rulers of Mesopotamian political history. For the first time in Babylonian history, foreigners controlled the country without assimilating its culture, and the region became a province in a large empire whose center was outside the borders of Mesopotamia.

For Further Reading

Resources listed here will guide the reader in learning more about the Babylonians. Advanced students will find complete bibliographic details for much of the primary and original-language sources in the notes, as well as more on the secondary literature. The last portion of this annotated bibliography includes standard reference tools as well as a few selected critical editions of texts in translation related to the study of the Babylonians.

Brinkman, John A. *A Political History of Post-Kassite Babylonia, 1158–722 B.C.* AnOr 43. Rome: Pontifical Biblical Institute, 1968. The definitive study of this period, based on primary sources with rigorous assessment of their historical value. All studies of the Babylonians during this time frame must begin with this volume.

Hallo, William W., and William K. Simpson. *The Ancient Near East: A History.* 2nd ed. Fort Worth: Harcourt Brace College Publishers, 1998. A complete history of the ancient Near East in two parts. Part 1 covers Mesopotamia and the Asiatic Near East, written by Hallo, while part 2 is devoted to Egypt and supplied by Simpson. Authoritative and well written, this book has been a popular introduction to the ancient Near East since it first appeared in 1971.

Jacobsen, Thorkild. *The Treasures of Darkness: A History of Mesopotamian Religion.* New Haven: Yale University Press, 1976. Traces the history of Mesopotamian religion through four thousand years of development, in which the gods were perceived first as providers for the necessities of life, then as protectors against enemies, next as parents with whom personal relationships were possible, and, finally, in the first millennium B.C.E., as cruel warriors. Should be read in conjunction with A. Leo Oppenheim (see below).

Kramer, Samuel N. *History Begins at Sumer: Thirty-Nine Firsts in Man's Recorded History.* 3rd ed. Philadelphia: University of Philadelphia Press, 1981. An important introduction to the topics covered in chapter 2 of this book. Kramer discusses the important innovations of the Sumerian precursors of the Babylonians during the third and early second millennia B.C.E. Good first book on the topic.

Kuhrt, Amélie. *The Ancient Near East, c. 3000–330 BC.* 2 vols. London: Routledge, 1994. Authoritative and well written, this two-volume work covers an enormous amount of material. After a fifteen-page introduction, the author goes through the history of the ancient Near East chronologically from the development of states and cities (3000–1600 B.C.E.), to the "Great Powers" (1600–1050 B.C.E.), and finally to political transformation and the great empires (1200–330 B.C.E.). In each section the author alternates between Mesopotamia, Egypt, and, where pertinent, Syria-Palestine and Anatolia.

Leick, Gwendolyn. *The Babylonians: An Introduction.* London: Routledge, 2002. General introduction with an anthropological slant. After an introduction dealing with geography, literacy, and the role of writing, the author includes chapters on political history, the social and economic structure of Babylonian society, religion, and material culture.

Nemet-Nejat, Karen R. *Daily Life in Ancient Mesopotamia.* Westport, Conn.: Greenwood, 1998. After general discussions of geography and history, this volume covers topics such as writing, education and the production of literature, the sciences, recreation, religion, government, and economy, as well as discussions of family life in the city and country. May be used as a reference tool but also reads well as an introduction.

Oates, Joan. *Babylon.* 2nd ed. New York: Thames & Hudson, 1986. Helpful introduction from a textual and archaeological perspective. Traces the political history generally and concludes with a comprehensive chapter on the "legacy of Babylon."

Oppenheim, A. Leo. *Ancient Mesopotamia: Portrait of a Dead Civilization.* Rev. ed. Chicago: University of Chicago Press, 1977. Classic treatment of ancient Mesopotamian culture and society. Particularly important is the author's approach to Mesopotamian religion, which he believes "cannot and should not be written" because of a lack of available evidence and because of the tremendous conceptual and cultural barriers that separate Western thinking from such an ancient polytheistic religion. Should be read in conjunction with the works of Thorkild Jacobsen.

Postgate, J. Nicholas. *Early Mesopotamia: Society and Economy at the Dawn of History.* London: Routledge, 1992. Authoritative study of ancient Mesopotamia from 3000 to 1500 B.C.E. The book focuses on southern Mesopotamia, the alluvial Tigris and Euphrates plain, because of its cultural continuity, the amount of material available, and the contributions of the region to human history. The author considers 1500 B.C.E. to be a major cultural and political hiatus, dividing

Mesopotamian political history into distinct halves. Thus the Old Babylonian world is deeply rooted in the third millennium, while Kassite culture is more akin to the first.

Potts, Daniel T. *Mesopotamian Civilization: The Material Foundations.* Ithaca, N.Y.: Cornell University Press, 1997. A useful collection of stand-alone essays covering features of Mesopotamian civilization often overlooked in other studies. Gives much attention to the written cuneiform sources while also updating and interacting with the pertinent secondary literature.

Roaf, Michael. *Cultural Atlas of Mesopotamia and the Ancient Near East.* New York: Facts on File, 1996. The best available atlas on ancient Mesopotamia. Also includes much discussion and treatment of relevant background information.

Roux, Georges. *Ancient Iraq.* 3rd ed. London: Penguin, 1992. Written by a French medical doctor who subsequently became a scholar of ancient Mesopotamia in his own right and published articles in technical journals. A comprehensive survey with an astounding sweep from Paleolithic times to the Sassanians (224–651 C.E.), this book is engagingly written and lucid. Its usefulness is still evident in its third edition since its original publication in 1964.

Saggs, H. W. F. *The Greatness That Was Babylon: A Survey of the Ancient Civilization of the Tigris-Euphrates Valley.* 2nd ed. London: Sidgwick & Jackson, 1988. Originally published in 1962, this authoritative and comprehensive treatment covers Babylonian society, law and administration, trade and economics, religion, literature, and science, as well as providing an overview of political history. Abbreviated and more up-to-date treatment may be found in the author's *Babylonians* (Berkeley and Los Angeles: University of California Press, 2000).

Snell, Daniel C. *Life in the Ancient Near East, 3100–332 B.C.E.* New Haven: Yale University Press, 1997. More than is typically found in the "everyday life" genre, this volume covers the entire ancient world chronologically from the origin of cities (5500 B.C.E.) to the fall of the Persians (332 B.C.E.). Chapters devoted to politically defined periods of time cover what may be called a social and economic history, focusing especially on Mesopotamia but including Egypt where possible. An interesting feature is the way each chapter begins with an imaginative re-creation of the lives of real people attested in a specific text from the period covered in that chapter.

Soden, Wolfram von. *The Ancient Orient: An Introduction to the Study of the Ancient Near East.* Grand Rapids: Eerdmans, 1994. A general introduction by a leading philologist. Surveys the cuneiform cultures of ancient Western Asia, namely, Assyria and Babylonia, early northern Syria, and at times Elam in the southeast and Urartu in the north.

Van De Mieroop, Marc. *Cuneiform Texts and the Writing of History.* London: Routledge, 1999. An introduction to the written sources from ancient Mesopotamia. Surveys the variety of texts written in cuneiform script and their challenges in re-creating ancient history. Explores the role of cuneiform sources in reconstructing political history but includes especially social and economic history as well.

Walker, C. B. F. *Cuneiform.* Reading the Past 3. London: British Museum; Berkeley and Los Angeles: University of California Press, 1987. Although brief, this volume surveys the cuneiform writing system from its earliest logographic signs to the last astronomical tablets (approximately 3000 B.C.E. to 75 C.E.). Includes discussion of the origins and development of cuneiform, the nature of writing on tablets and monuments, and the role of scribes and libraries in ancient Mesopotamian culture.

Wiseman, Donald J. *Nebuchadrezzar and Babylon.* The Schweich Lectures 1983. Oxford: Published for the British Academy by Oxford University Press, 1985. A study of Nebuchadnezzar II (605–562 B.C.E.). Relies on archaeology and texts, especially the Neo-Babylonian Chronicles, to survey the man himself and the city of Babylon, then explores biblical and Hellenistic connections.

Texts and Reference Works

Chavalas, Mark W., ed. *The Ancient Near East: Historical Sources in Translation.* Oxford: Blackwell, forthcoming. When available, this volume will present all the pertinent historical texts from the ancient Near East in contemporary English translation.

Dalley, Stephanie. *Myths from Mesopotamia: Creation, the Flood, Gilgamesh, and Others.* 2nd ed. Oxford: Oxford University Press, 2000. Recent excellent translations of the Atra-ḫasis Epic, the Gilgamesh Epic, the Descent of Ishtar, Adapa, the *Enūma Eliš,* and others. The translator included helpful introductions to each text and notes on the translations themselves.

Ebeling, Erich, et al. *Reallexikon der Assyriologie und vorderasiatischen Archäologie.* 16 vols. Berlin: de Gruyter, 1928–. Abbreviated as *RlA,* this encyclopedia contains authoritative articles on nearly every topic related to all cultures using cuneiform script (Mesopotamia, North Syria, and Anatolia), from the fourth to the first millennia B.C.E. Of the sixteen volumes planned, ten are now available. The earlier ones are now quite dated, but later volumes are valuable for any study of the Babylonians.

Edwards, I. E. S., and John Boardman, eds. *The Cambridge Ancient History*. 14 vols. Cambridge: Cambridge University Press, 1970–. Abbreviated here and known by students of ancient history as *CAH*, the *Cambridge Ancient History* is a complete and authoritative history of the ancient world in fourteen volumes, the first six of which are essential to any study of the Babylonians. Originally published as twelve volumes (1924–39), new editions were launched in 1970. Volumes I/1, I/2, II/1, and II/2 (3rd ed., 1970–75) are still useful although now somewhat dated, while volumes III/1, III/2, III/3, and IV (2nd ed., 1982–91) are indispensable for any study of the Babylonians.

Foster, Benjamin R. *From Distant Days: Myths, Tales, and Poetry of Ancient Mesopotamia*. Bethesda, Md.: CDL Press, 1995. An abridgment and rearrangement of the author's two-volume work *Before the Muses: An Anthology of Akkadian Literature* (Potomac, Md.: CDL Press, 1993). This volume is devoted to Akkadian literary texts and includes a helpful introduction to Akkadian literature in general.

George, Andrew. *The Epic of Gilgamesh: The Babylonian Epic Poem and Other Texts in Akkadian and Sumerian*. London: Penguin, 2003. Wonderful translation in contemporary English by a leading Assyriologist. The volume has a helpful forty-page introduction, followed by translations of the Standard Version of the Babylonian Gilgamesh Epic, earlier Babylonian versions, and the Sumerian poems of Gilgamesh.

Grayson, A. K. *Assyrian and Babylonian Chronicles*. TCS 5. Locust Valley, N.Y.: Augustin; 1975. Repr., Winona Lake, Ind.: Eisenbrauns, 2000. Standard text-critical edition of all Mesopotamian chronicles available in 1975. Contains important introductions and commentary on the texts. Needs now to be supplemented by Jean-Jacques Glassner, *Mesopotamian Chronicles* (ed. Benjamin R. Foster; SBLWAW 19; Atlanta: Society of Biblical Literature, 2004).

Hallo, William W., and K. L. Younger, eds. *The Context of Scripture*. 3 vols. Leiden: Brill, 1997–2002. Abbreviated here as *COS*. These volumes contain fresh translations of many of the pertinent texts, although some are only excerpted. Most also have commentary in the notes or introductions. Volume 1 contains the so-called canonical compositions, volume 2 offers monumental inscriptions, and volume 3 includes archival documents.

Kaiser, Otto, and Riekele Borger, eds. *Texte aus der Umwelt des Alten Testaments*. 3 vols. Gütersloh: Mohn, 1982–97. Abbreviated here as *TUAT*. Recent translations of almost all relevant texts. Volume 1 contains legal and economic documents, as well as historical and chronological texts. Volume 2 has all the pertinent religious texts, and volume 3 wisdom literature, myths, and epics.

Pritchard, James B., ed. *Ancient Near Eastern Texts Relating to the Old Testament*. 3rd ed. with supplement. Princeton, N.J.: Princeton University Press, 1969. Abbreviated here as *ANET*. Contains translations of many of the most important cuneiform texts related to the study of the Babylonians. Although many of the translations are now dated and the volume must therefore be used with care, this collection has the advantage of housing in one location large selections of the texts for easy access by the student.

Roth, Martha T. *Law Collections from Mesopotamia and Asia Minor*. 2nd ed. SBLWAW 6. Atlanta: Scholars Press, 1997. Text-critical edition of all available legal material. After an introduction, the Sumerian and Akkadian legal collections are presented in transcription and translation. The Hittite laws are translated by Harry A. Hoffner, although without the transcriptions.

Sasson, Jack M., ed. *Civilizations of the Ancient Near East*. 4 vols. New York: Scribner, 1995. Repr. in 2 vols., Peabody, Mass.: Hendrickson, 2000. Abbreviated here as *CANE,* this thorough treatment covers everything from the ancient Near East in Western thought to the visual and performing arts in the ancient world. Fresh and authoritative essays on nearly every topic imaginable. Volume 2 is on the history and culture of the ancient Near East and is essential for any student of the Babylonians, but the other three volumes also contain much of importance. This resource supplements and even replaces a few of the older volumes of *CAH*.

NOTES

PREFACE

1. For the dates used here, see John A. Brinkman, "Mesopotamian Chronology of the Historical Period," in A. Leo Oppenheim, *Ancient Mesopotamia: Portrait of a Dead Civilization* (rev. ed.; Chicago: University of Chicago Press, 1977), 335–48; see also M. B. Rowton, "Chronology, II. Ancient Western Asia," *CAH*³ 1/1:193-239; and Frederick H. Cryer, "Chronology: Issues and Problems," *CANE* 2:651–64, esp. 656–59.

2. Hermann Gasche, *Dating the Fall of Babylon: A Reappraisal of Second-Millennium Chronology* (Mesopotamian History and Environment 4; Chicago: University of Ghent and the Oriental Institute of the University of Chicago, 1998); Julian Reade, "Assyrian King-Lists, the Royal Tombs of Ur, and Indus Origins," *JNES* 60 (2001): 1–29.

3. "Note on the Calendar," *CAH*² 3/2:750.

CHAPTER 1

1. So, for example, Ur-Nammu, the founder of a Sumerian empire at the southern city of Ur in the late third millennium B.C.E., assumed the title "King of Sumer and Akkad" once he ruled as far north as Nippur, in order to indicate his hegemony over a unified southern and central Mesopotamia (see ch. 2); see William W. Hallo, *Early Mesopotamian Royal Titles: A Philologic and Historical Analysis* (AOS 43; New Haven: American Oriental Society, 1957), 77–88.

2. In texts from the first millennium, the principal watercourse flowing through Babylon is sometimes the Araḫtum, which rejoins the Euphrates further downstream; at other times the Euphrates and the Araḫtum are both said to pass through the city; see John A. Brinkman, *Prelude to Empire: Babylonian Society and Politics, 747–626 B.C.* (Occasional Publications of the Babylonian Fund 7; Philadelphia: Distributed by Babylonian Fund, University Museum, 1984), 67 n. 318.

3. Ignace J. Gelb, "The Name of Babylon," *Journal of the Institute of Asian Studies* 1 (1955): 1–4; Burkhart Kienast, "The Name of the City of Babylon," *Sumer* 35 (1979): 246–48.

4. Gelb, "Name of Babylon," 3–4.

5. A. R. George, *Babylonian Topographical Texts* (OLA 40; Leuven: Departement Oriëntalistiek, Uitgeverij Peeters, 1992), 7.

6. John A. Brinkman, "Karduniaš," *RlA* 5:423.

7. The valley is a relatively recent geological creation formed by the alluvial deposit of the rivers in the trench between the Arabian Desert to the west and the mountains of Iran to the east; see J. Nicholas Postgate, *Early Mesopotamia: Society and Economy at the Dawn of History* (London: Routledge, 1992), 6; Robert M. Adams, *The Heartland of Cities: Surveys of Ancient Settlement and Land Use on the Central Floodplain of the Euphrates* (Chicago: University of Chicago Press, 1981), 14–19.

8. Postgate, *Early Mesopotamia,* 6–7.

9. Artificial irrigation in the alluvial plain resulted in crop yields higher than possible anywhere else in the ancient world. Less land was therefore required around larger settlements, making urbanization possible; see Hans J. Nissen, "Western Asia before the Age of Empires," *CANE* 2:791–806, esp. 798.

10. Adams, *Heartland of Cities,* 52–129; Michael Roaf, *Cultural Atlas of Mesopotamia and the Ancient Near East* (New York: Facts on File, 1996), 58–69.

11. Adams, *Heartland of Cities,* 60–81; Hans J. Nissen, *The Early History of the Ancient Near East, 9000–2000 B.C.* (trans. Elizabeth Lutzeier and Kenneth J. Northcott; Chicago: University of Chicago Press, 1988), 56–127; Henri Frankfort, "The Last Predynastic Period in Babylonia," *CAH*³ 1/2: 71–92, esp. 71–81; on the use of colonies at this early stage for purposes of acquiring stone and wood, rare commodities in southern Mesopotamia, through trade, see Guillermo Algaze, *The Uruk World System: The Dynamics of Early Mesopotamian Civilization* (Chicago: University of Chicago Press, 1993), 110–27.

12. For summary of the Samarran, 'Oueili, and Ubaid cultures prior to the Early Uruk period in southern Mesopotamia, see Amélie Kuhrt, *The Ancient Near East, c. 3000–330 BC* (2 vols.; London: Routledge, 1994), 1:21–22.

13. Max E. L. Mallowan, "The Early Dynastic Period in Mesopotamia," *CAH*³ 1/2: 238–314, esp. 272–90.

14. McGuire Gibson, *The City and Area of Kish* (ed. Henry Field and Edith M. Laird; Miami: Field Research Projects, 1972); Robert M. Adams and Hans J. Nissen, *The Uruk Countryside: The Natural Setting of Urban Societies* (Chicago: University of Chicago Press, 1972), 42.

15. Marc Van De Mieroop, *Cuneiform Texts and the Writing of History* (London: Routledge, 1999), 11; similarly, C. B. F. Walker, *Cuneiform* (Reading the Past 3; London: British Museum; Berkeley and Los Angeles: University of California Press, 1987), 38.

16. As has been suggested by Daniel C. Snell, *Life in the Ancient Near East, 3100–332 B.C.E.* (New Haven: Yale University Press, 1997), 8–10.

17. Bruce G. Trigger, *A History of Archaeological Thought* (Cambridge: Cambridge University Press, 1989), esp. 73–79; Israel Finkelstein, "Toward a New Periodization and Nomenclature of the Archaeology of the Southern Levant," in *The Study of the Ancient Near East in The Twenty-First Century: The William Foxwell Albright Centennial Conference* (ed. Jerrold S. Cooper and Glenn M. Schwartz; Winona Lake, Ind.: Eisenbrauns, 1996), 102–23, esp. 104–9.

18. A. K. Grayson, "History and Culture of Babylonia," *ABD* 4:755–77, esp. 758.

19. On the spelling of his name, see ch. 2.

20. A point emphasized by Snell, *Life in the Ancient Near East,* 5.

21. *Atbash* is visual wordplay in which the first letter of the alphabet is used as a substitute for the last, the second letter for the penultimate letter, and so forth; see Jack M. Sasson, "Wordplay in the OT," *IDBSup,* 968–70, esp. 969.

22. David S. Vanderhooft, *The Neo-Babylonian Empire and Babylon in the Latter Prophets* (HSM 59; Cambridge: Harvard Semitic Museum, 1999), esp. 115–202.

23. Bill T. Arnold and David B. Weisberg, "A Centennial Review of Friedrich Delitzsch's 'Babel und Bibel' Lectures," *JBL* 121 (2002): 441–57.

24. William W. Hallo, "Compare and Contrast: The Contextual Approach to Biblical Literature," in *The Bible in the Light of Cuneiform Literature* (ed. William W. Hallo, Bruce W. Jones, and Gerald L. Mattingly; Scripture in Context 3; Ancient Near Eastern Texts and Studies 8; Lewiston, N.Y.: Mellen, 1990), 1–30; Karel van der Toorn, *Sin and Sanction in Israel and Mesopotamia: A Comparative Study* (SSN 22; Assen: Van Gorcum, 1985), 1–9.

25. Walker, *Cuneiform,* 48–52; Roaf, *Cultural Atlas of Mesopotamia,* 152–53; Thorkild Jacobsen, "Searching for Sumer and Akkad," *CANE* 4:2743–52.

26. For more on the Greek historians discussed here, see Amélie Kuhrt, "Ancient Mesopotamia in Classical Greek and Hellenistic Thought," *CANE* 1:55–65.

27. Kuhrt states that the two kings named Labynetus represent Nebuchadnezzar and Nabonidus ("Ancient Mesopotamia," 60). Others assume that Herodotus was simply mistaken in assuming Labynetus was the son of a king by the same name (T. F. R. G. Braun, "The Greeks in the Near East," *CAH*² 3/3:1–31, esp. 23).

28. Stanley M. Burstein, *The Babyloniaca of Berossus* (Sources and Monographs on the Ancient Near East 1/5; Malibu, Calif.: Undena Publications, 1978).

29. Roaf, *Cultural Atlas of Mesopotamia,* 14.

30. William W. Hallo, "The Concept of Canonicity in Cuneiform and Biblical Literature: A Comparative Appraisal," in *The Biblical Canon in Comparative Perspective* (ed. K. Lawson Younger Jr., William W. Hallo, and Bernard F. Batto; Scripture in Context 4; Ancient Near Eastern Texts and Studies 11; Lewiston, N.Y.: Mellen, 1991), 1–19; Erica Reiner, "First-Millennium Babylonian Literature," *CAH*² 3/2:293–321; Oppenheim, *Ancient Mesopotamia,* 13–18.

31. Oppenheim, *Ancient Mesopotamia,* 13; Wolfram von Soden, "Das Problem der zeitlichen Einordnung akkadischer Literaturwerke," *MDOG* 85 (1953): 14–26.

32. Reiner, "First-Millennium Babylonian Literature," esp. 294–95.

33. K. R. Veenhof, *Cuneiform Archives and Libraries: Papers Read at the 30ᵉ Rencontre Assyriologique Internationale, Leiden, 4–8 July 1983* (Uitgaven van het Nederlands Historisch-Archaeologisch Instituut te Istanbul 52; Istanbul: Nederlands Historisch-Archaeologisch Instituut te Istanbul, 1986).

34. A. K. Grayson, "Assyrian Civilization," *CAH*² 3/2:194–228, esp. 228.

35. For translation and interpretation, see ibid., esp. 227. Neo-Assyrian administrative records at Nineveh itemized lists of literary works confiscated from Babylonia, apparently just after Ashurbanipal captured Babylon in 648 B.C.E. (Simo Parpola, "Assyrian Library Records," *JNES* 42 [1983]: 1–29, esp. 1–12).

36. Warwick Ball and Jeremy A. Black, "Excavations in Iraq, 1985–1986," *Iraq* 49 (1987): under "Sippar."

37. Oppenheim, *Ancient Mesopotamia,* 13–18; Reiner, "First-Millennium Babylonian Literature," esp. 295; Walker, *Cuneiform,* 38–39.

38. Van De Mieroop, *Cuneiform Texts,* 13–38.

CHAPTER 2

1. He claimed that numerous features of human civilization—including writing—emerged first at Sumer; see Samuel N. Kramer, *History Begins at Sumer: Thirty-Nine Firsts in Man's Recorded History* (3rd ed.; Philadelphia: University of Philadelphia Press, 1981).

2. Many archaeologist have identified another cultural layer toward the close of the Late Uruk period, the so-called Jemdet Nasr period (3000–2900 B.C.E.); see Henri Frankfort, "Last Predynastic Period in Babylonia," 71–92. However, the features of this archaeological period are closely associated with the previous Uruk period, and it may simply be a regional style of pottery and art isolated in southern Mesopotamia.

3. Jean-Jacques Glassner, Zainab Bahrani, and Marc Van de Mieroop, *Writing in Sumer: The Invention of Cuneiform* (Baltimore: Johns Hopkins University Press, 2003); Walker, *Cuneiform,* 7–12.

4. A process apparently involving recording practices using at first hollow clay balls with seal impressions (or "bullae") and small clay balls inside, followed then by bullae with impressions on the outer surface, and finally by clay tablets with the markings and seals on the surface; see Postgate, *Early Mesopotamia,* 52–54; Denise Schmandt-Besserat, "Tokens at Uruk," *BaghM* 19 (1988): 1–175.

5. Jerrold S. Cooper, *Presargonic Inscriptions* (Sumerian and Akkadian Royal Inscriptions 1; New Haven: American Oriental Society, 1986), 3–4 and 14; Cooper, *Reconstructing History from Ancient Inscriptions: The Lagash-Umma Border Conflict* (Malibu, Calif.: Undena Publications, 1983), esp. 19–21. The Sumerian King List (see below), although useful in general, cannot be relied upon for a chronological outline of the period.

6. Frederick H. Cryer, "Chronology," 651–64, esp. 660; for archaeological criteria for these divisions, the older work by Mallowan is still useful (Max E. L. Mallowan, "The Early Dynastic Period in Mesopotamia," *CAH*³ 1/2: 238–314, esp. 238–46).

7. Åke W. Sjöberg and Eugen Bergmann, *The Collection of the Sumerian Temple Hymns* (TCS 3; Locust Valley, N.Y.: Augustin, 1969), 5–154.

8. Jean-Jacques Glassner, *Mesopotamian Chronicles* (ed. Benjamin R. Foster; WAW 19; Atlanta: Society of Biblical Literature, 2004), 117–26; A. L. Oppenheim, "Texts from the Beginnings to the First Dynasty of Babylon," *ANET*, 265–69, esp. 265–66; Thorkild Jacobsen, *The Sumerian King List* (AS 11; Chicago: University of Chicago Press, 1939); Walter Beyerlin, *Near Eastern Religious Texts Relating to the Old Testament* (OTL; Philadelphia: Westminster, 1978), 87–89; for the nature of the king list, see Piotr Michalowski, "History as Charter: Some Observations on the Sumerian King List," *JAOS* 103 (1983): 237–48.

9. Thus in the view of the King List this great flood, which nearly destroyed humankind, is the event separating the Uruk period (or, the Jemdet Nasr period) from the Early Dynastic period (Max E. L. Mallowan, "Noah's Flood Reconsidered," *Iraq* 26 [1964]: 62–82).

10. J. Nicholas Postgate, "Royal Ideology and State Administration in Sumer and Akkad," *CANE* 1:395–411.

11. Mallowan's list of the principal sites is still useful ("Early Dynastic Period," 272–90); for more on what follows in this paragraph, see Postgate, "Royal Ideology and State Administration," esp. 396–400; and Walter R. Bodine, "Sumerians," in *Peoples of the Old Testament World* (ed. Alfred J. Hoerth, Gerald L. Mattingly, and Edwin M. Yamauchi; Grand Rapids: Baker, 1994), 19–42, esp. 27–33.

12. In two influential articles Jacobsen proposed the presence in Early Dynastic times of a bicameral system in which an upper house of "elders" and a lower house of "free men" acted by consensus in reaching decisions; see Thorkild Jacobsen, "Primitive Democracy in Ancient Mesopotamia," *JNES* 2 (1943): 159–72; Jacobsen, "Early Political Development in Mesopotamia," *ZA* 52 (1957): 91–140.

13. Postgate, *Early Mesopotamia,* 33–34.

14. John F. Robertson, "The Social and Economic Organization of Ancient Mesopotamian Temples," *CANE* 1:443–54.

15. Postgate, *Early Mesopotamia,* 109–36.

16. Daniel T. Potts, *Mesopotamian Civilization: The Material Foundations* (Ithaca, N.Y.: Cornell University Press, 1997), 211.

17. Postgate, *Early Mesopotamia,* 28–31.

18. M.-J. Seux, "Les titres royaux *šar kiššati* et *šar kibrāt arbaʾi*," *RA* 59 (1965): 1–18.

19. On his name as either "Uruʾinimgina" or "Urukagina," see G. J. Selz, "Zum Namen des Herrschers URU-INIM-GI-NA(-K): Ein neuer Deutungsvorschlag," *NABU* 44 (1992): 34–36.

20. Cooper, *Presargonic Inscriptions,* 70–78; William W. Hallo, "Reforms of Uru-inimgina," *COS* 2.152:407–8.

21. For a succinct summary of the literary compositions rehearsing his exploits, see Bodine, "Sumerians," 29–30.

22. Cooper, *Presargonic Inscriptions,* 18; Dietz O. Edzard, "Mebaragesi," *RlA* 7:614; Maureen G. Kovacs, *The Epic of Gilgamesh* (Stanford, Calif.: Stanford University Press, 1989), xi; Jeffrey H. Tigay, *The Evolution of the Gilgamesh Epic* (Philadelphia: University of Pennsylvania Press, 1982), 13–16; Dietz O. Edzard, "Enmebaragesi von Kiš," *ZA* 53 (1959): 9–26.

23. Edmond Sollberger, "The Tummal Inscription," *JCS* 16 (1962): 40–47.

24. Adam Falkenstein, "Gilgameš," *RlA* 3:357–63.

25. Robert D. Biggs, "Semitic Names in the Fara Period," *Or* 36 (1967): 55–66; Jerrold S. Cooper, "Sumerian and Akkadian in Sumer and Akkad," *Or* 42 (1973): 239–46.

26. For the former, see Ignace J. Gelb, "Ebla and the Kish Civilization," in *La Lingua Di Ebla: Atti Del Convegno Internazionale (Napoli, 21–23 Aprile 1980)* (ed. Luigi Cagni; Istituto universitario orientale: Seminario di studi asiatici, Series Minor 14; Napoli: Istituto universitario orientale, 1981), 9–73, esp. 52–57; and Robert D. Biggs, "Ebla and Abu Salabikh: The Linguistic and Literary Aspects," in Cagni, *La Lingua Di Ebla,* 121–33, esp. 122–24. For the latter, see Simo Parpola, "Proto-Assyrian," in *Wirtschaft Und Gesellschaft von Ebla: Akten der Internationalen Tagung, Heidelberg, 4.–7. November 1986* (ed. Hartmut Waetzoldt and Harald Hauptmann; Heidelberger Studien zum alten Orient 2; Heidelberg: Heidelberger Orientverlag, 1988), 293–98. Prior to the discovery of Ebla, scholars could confidently state that the Old Akkadian dialect of Sargon I was "the first time a Semitic language had ever been written"; see C. J. Gadd, "The Dynasty of Agade and the Gutian Invasion," *CAH*[3] 1/2:417–63, esp. 450–51.

27. There appears to be no racial tension between Semites and Sumerians, at least according to the nearly equal number of Semitic personal names compared to Sumerian. Military conflict between the two appears motivated by factors other than ethnic differences; see Thorkild Jacobsen, *Toward the Image of Tammuz and Other Essays on Mesopotamian History and Culture* (HSS 21; Cambridge: Harvard University Press, 1970), 187–92.

28. Marie-Louise Thomsen, *The Sumerian Language: An Introduction to Its History and Grammatical Structure* (Copenhagen Studies in Assyriology, Mesopotamia 10; Copenhagen: Akademisk Forlag, 1984), 15–20.

29. John Huehnergard, *A Grammar of Akkadian* (HSS 45; Winona Lake, Ind.: Eisenbrauns, 2000), xxi–xxvi.

30. Postgate, *Early Mesopotamia,* 38–40; Snell, *Life in the Ancient Near East,* 18, 33, 168 n. 5.

31. Douglas Frayne, *Sargonic and Gutian Periods, 2334–2113 BC* (RIM 2; Toronto: University of Toronto Press, 1993), 11–12, text E2.1.1.1, lines 79–85; Ignace J. Gelb and Burkhart Kienast, *Die altakkadischen Königsinschriften des dritten Jahrtausends v. Chr* (Freiburger altorientalische Studien 7; Stuttgart: Steiner, 1990), 157–63.

32. Sabina Franke, "Kings of Akkad: Sargon and Naram-Sin," *CANE* 2:831–41, esp. 832.

33. Joan G. Westenholz, *Legends of the Kings of Akkade: The Texts* (Mesopotamian Civilizations 7; Winona Lake, Ind.: Eisenbrauns, 1997); Gadd, "Dynasty of Agade," 450.

34. Marvin A. Powell, "Metrology and Mathematics in Ancient Mesopotamia," *CANE* 3:1941–57, esp. 1955–56.

35. In addition to Sjöberg and Bergmann, *Collection of the Sumerian Temple Hymns,* see Åke W. Sjöberg, "In-nin šàgur₄-ra: A Hymn to the Goddess Inanna by the en-Priestess Enḫeduanna," *ZA* 65 (1975): 161–253; William W. Hallo, "The Exaltation of Inanna," *COS* 1.160:518–22; and William W. Hallo and J. J. A. van Dijk, *The Exaltation of Inanna* (Yale Near Eastern Researches 3; New Haven: Yale University Press, 1968).

36. Westenholz, *Legends of the Kings of Akkade,* esp. 173–368.

37. Hallo, *Early Mesopotamian Royal Titles,* 49–56.

38. Burkhart Kienast, "Inscription of Narām-sîn: Deification of the King," *COS* 2.90:244; see also William W. Hallo, "They Requested Him as God of Their City: A Classical Moment in the Mesopotamian Experience," in *The Classical Moment: Views From Seven Literatures* (ed. Gail Holst-Warhaft and David R. McCann; Lanham, Md.: Rowman & Littlefield, 1999), 22–35.

39. Hallo, *Early Mesopotamian Royal Titles,* 59.

40. Postgate, *Early Mesopotamia,* 266–69.

41. Kuhrt, *Ancient Near East,* 2:661.

42. On the so-called *narû* literature, see Joan Goodnick-Westenholz, "Heroes of Akkad," *JAOS* 103 (1983): 327–36, esp. 327–28.

43. Brian Lewis, *The Sargon Legend: A Study of the Akkadian Text and the Tale of the Hero Who Was Exposed at Birth* (ASOR Dissertation Series 4; Cambridge: American Schools of Oriental Research, 1980).

44. Infatuation with Sargon's accomplishments resulted in the use of his name by an early king of Assyria (Sargon I, twentieth century B.C.E.) and again by the celebrated Sargon II in the eighth century (721–705 B.C.E.).

45. Benjamin R. Foster, "The Birth Legend of Sargon of Akkad," *COS* 1.133:461; E. A. Speiser, "The Legend of Sargon," *ANET,* 119.

46. As in the Weidner Chronicle; see Bill T. Arnold, "The Weidner Chronicle," in *The Ancient Near East: Historical Sources in Translation* (ed. Mark W. Chavalas; Oxford: Blackwell, forthcoming); Alan R. Millard, "The Weidner Chronicle," *COS* 1.138:468–70; Glassner, *Mesopotamian Chronicles,* 263–69; for the Curse of Akkad, see Jerrold S. Cooper, *The Curse of Agade* (Baltimore: Johns Hopkins University Press, 1983).

47. Mario Liverani, *Akkad, the First World Empire: Structure, Ideology, Traditions* (History of the Ancient Near East 5; Padova: Sargon, 1993).

48. Gadd, "Dynasty of Agade," esp. 451–52; and see Pierre Amiet, *Art in the Ancient World: A Handbook of Styles and Forms* (New York: Rizzoli, 1981), 74 and 106.

49. Oppenheim, "Texts from the Beginnings," esp. 265–66; Jacobsen, *Sumerian King List,* 113–15, line vii 1–7; Glassner, *Mesopotamian Chronicles,* 123–25.

50. Dietz O. Edzard, *Gudea and His Dynasty* (RIM 3/1; Toronto: University of Toronto Press, 1997); Richard E. Averbeck, "The Cylinders of Gudea," *COS* 2.155:417–33.

51. On the chronological problems, see M. B. Rowton, "Chronology, II. Ancient Western Asia," *CAH*³ 1/1:193–239, esp. 219. On the Gutians, see William W. Hallo, "Gutium," *RlA* 3:708–20; Gadd, "Dynasty of Agade," 458.

52. Gadd, "Dynasty of Agade," 462. The Weidner Chronicle says simply that Utu-ḫegal failed to care for Marduk's city (i.e., Babylon), "so the river carried off his corpse"; see Arnold, "Weidner Chronicle"; Millard, "Weidner Chronicle," 469; Glassner, *Mesopotamian Chronicles,* 269.

53. C. J. Gadd, "Babylonia, c. 2120–1800 B.C.," *CAH*³ 1/2:595–643, esp. 595–623; Kuhrt, *Ancient Near East,* 1:56–73; and especially on Ur III administration and economy, see Piotr Michalowski, "Charisma and Control: On Continuity and Change in Early Mesopotamian Bureaucratic Systems," in *The Organization of Power: Aspects of Bureaucracy in the Ancient Near East* (ed. Robert D. Biggs and McGuire Gibson; Studies in Ancient Oriental Civilization 46; Chicago: Oriental Institute of the University of Chicago, 1991), 55–68; Piotr Steinkeller, "The Administrative and Economic Organization of the Ur III State: The Core and the Periphery," in Biggs and Gibson, *Organization of Power,* 19–42.

54. Douglas Frayne, *Ur III Period, 2112–2004 BC* (RIM 3/2; Toronto: University of Toronto Press, 1997), 35, text E3/2.1.1.12, line 9, and see page 12 for discussion.

55. Roaf, *Cultural Atlas of Mesopotamia,* 104–7; Elizabeth C. Stone, "Ziggurat," *OEANE* 5:390–91.

56. The number of Neo-Sumerian administrative texts is larger than all the other periods of Mesopotamian history put together; see Walker, *Cuneiform,* 17.

57. Jacob Klein, "Shulgi of Ur: King of a Neo-Sumerian Empire," *CANE* 2:843–57, esp. 844.

58. Jacob Klein, *The Royal Hymns of Shulgi, King of Ur: Man's Quest for Immortal Fame* (Transactions of the American Philosophical Society 71/7; Philadelphia: American Philosophical Society, 1981).

59. In our discussion of these legal traditions, I will use "code" as has become conventional in the secondary literature, although these collections do not appear to have been referenced in the process of deciding cases in court, as the term would imply.

60. Martha T. Roth, *Law Collections from Mesopotamia and Asia Minor* (2nd ed.; WAW 6; Atlanta: Scholars Press, 1997), 13–22; Roth, "The Laws of Ur-Namma (Ur-Nammu)," *COS*

2.153:408–10. The debate on whether the code was from Ur-Nammu or Shulgi is focused on the literary style of the code's prologue and is not likely to be settled soon; see Fatma Yildiz, "A Tablet of Codex Ur-Nammu from Sippar," *Or* 50 (1981): 87–97; Samuel N. Kramer, "The Ur-Nammu Law Code: Who Was Its Author?" *Or* 52 (1983): 453–56; Piotr Michalowski and C. B. F. Walker, "A New Sumerian 'Law Code,'" in *Dumu-E2-Dub-Ba-a: Studies in Honor of Åke W. Sjöberg* (ed. Hermann Behrens, Darlene Loding, and Martha T. Roth; Occasional Publications of the Samuel Noah Kramer Fund 11; Philadelphia: Samuel Noah Kramer Fund, University Musum, 1989), 383–96, esp. 384–85.

61. Claus Wilcke, "Genealogical and Geographical Thought in the Sumerian King List," in Behrens, Loding, and Roth, *Dumu-E2-Dub-Ba-a*, 557–71, esp. 561–62.

62. For details of what follows, see Gadd, "Babylonia," esp. 607–17.

63. Arnold, "Weidner Chronicle"; Millard, "Weidner Chronicle," 469; Glassner, *Mesopotamian Chronicles*, 269.

64. Frayne, *Ur III Period*, 290–93.

65. William W. Hallo, "Lamentations and Prayers in Sumer and Akkad," *CANE* 3:1871–81, esp. 1879–80.

66. Gibson, *City and Area of Kish*, 37 n. 49.

67. This tradition is found in the Weidner Chronicle, lines 50–51 (see Arnold, "Weidner Chronicle"; Millard, "Weidner Chronicle," 469; Glassner, *Mesopotamian Chronicles*, 267) and in the Chronicle of Early Kings A, lines 18–19 (see A. K. Grayson, *Assyrian and Babylonian Chronicles* [TCS 5; Winona Lake, Ind.: Eisenbrauns, 2000], 149 and 153–54; Glassner, *Mesopotamian Chronicles*, 271). However, a recent copy of the Weidner Chronicle found at Sippar reverses Sargon's action, claiming he built a city opposite Babylon, which he named Akkad; see Farouk N. H. Al-Rawi, "Tablets from the Sippar Library I: The 'Weidner Chronicle': A Supposititious Royal Letter concerning a Vision," *Iraq* 52 (1990): 1–14: 10, line 18. On this tradition in the omen literature, see A. K. Grayson, "Divination and the Babylonian Chronicles," in *Rencontre Assyriologique Internationale, XIVth: La Divination en Mésopotamie Ancienne et dans les Régions Voisines* (Paris: Presses Universitaires de France, 1966), 73 n. 4; Gadd, "Dynasty of Agade," 419.

68. Frayne, *Sargonic and Gutian Periods*, 183; Johannes Renger, "The City of Babylon during the Old Babylonian Period," *Sumer* 35 (1979): 204–9, esp. 208.

69. Martha T. Roth, "The Laws of Hammurabi," *COS* 2.131:335–53, esp. 336; Roth, *Law Collections*, 76.

70. Benjamin R. Foster, "Epic of Creation," *COS* 1.111:390–402, esp. 400. The idea "Houses of the Great Gods" may be an etymological "translation" of Akkadian *bāb-ilim*, on which see Benno Landsberger and J. V. Kinnier Wilson, "The Fifth Tablet of the Enuma Elish," *JNES* 20 (1961): 154–79, esp. 178. On the name of "Babylon," see ch. 1 above.

71. On the etiological nature of Gen 11:9 in the narrative and the role of the wordplay, see Claus Westermann, *Genesis 1–11: A Commentary* (trans. John J. Scullion; Minneapolis: Augsburg, 1984), 553–54.

Chapter 3

1. Jean R. Kupper, *Les nomades en Mésopotamie au temps des rois de Mari* (Bibliothèque de la Faculté de philosophie et lettres de l'Université de Liège 142; Paris: Belles Lettres, 1957), 147–247; the review article by Ignace J. Gelb, "The Early History of the West Semitic Peoples," *JCS* 15 (1961): 27–47; Giorgio Buccellati, *The Amorites of the Ur III Period* (Pubblicazioni del Seminario di semitistica 1; Naples: Istituto orientale di Napoli, 1966).

2. Spelled mar-tu/tum^{ki} or mar-du^{ki}; the Ebla archives have yielded thirty attestations, dated to just before the Sargonic period. These occurrences apparently locate Amorites in mountain regions extending from Palmyra to the northeast up to the Euphrates (Alfonso

Archi, "Mardu in the Ebla Tablets," *Or* 54 [1985]: 7–13); on the use of *amurrû(m)* in Mari documents, see Jack M. Sasson, "About 'Mari and the Bible,'" *RA* 92 (1998): 97–123, esp. 121–23.

3. For summary of what we can know as it relates to the fourteenth and thirteenth centuries B.C.E., see Itamar Singer, "A Concise History of Amurru," in *Amurru Akkadian: A Linguistic Study* (ed. Shlomo Izre'el and Itamar Singer; HSS 40–41; 2 vols.; Atlanta: Scholars Press, 1991), 2:135–95; Moshe Anbar, *Les tribus amurrites de Mari* (OBO 108; Fribourg: Universitätsverlag; Göttingen: Vandenhoeck & Ruprecht, 1991); Robert M. Whiting, "Amorite Tribes and Nations of Second-Millennium Western Asia," *CANE* 2:1231–42.

4. Whiting, "Amorite Tribes and Nations," esp. 1233. For more on Amorite names and geographical distribution, see Ignace J. Gelb, J. Bartels, S.-M. Vance, and Robert M. Whiting, *Computer Aided Analysis of Amorite* (AS 21; Chicago: Oriental Institute of the University of Chicago, 1980).

5. For an early critique, see Sabatino Moscati, *The Semites in Ancient History: An Inquiry into the Settlement of the Beduin and Their Political Establishment* (Cardiff: University of Wales Press, 1959), 72–75.

6. Ilse Köhler-Rollefson, "A Model for the Development of Nomadic Pastoralism on the Transjordanian Plateau," in *Pastoralism in the Levant: Archaeological Materials in Anthropological Perspectives* (ed. Ofer Bar-Yosef and Anatoly M. Khazanov; Monographs in World Archaeology 10; Madison, Wis.: Prehistory Press, 1992), 11–18, esp. 11; see also the introductory chapter by the editors in the same volume, pp. 1–9; Victor H. Matthews, "Syria to the Early Second Millennium," in *Mesopotamia and the Bible: Comparative Explorations* (ed. Mark W. Chavalas and K. L. Younger; JSOTSup 341; London: Sheffield Academic Press, 2002), 168–90, esp. 172–77.

7. S. M. Voth, "Analysis of Military Titles and Functions in Published Texts of the Old Babylonian Period" (Ph.D. diss., Hebrew Union College, 1981), esp. 117–38 and 225–30; Phillipe Abrahami, "A propos des généraux (gal mar-tu) de la Mésopotamie du Nord à l'époque du règne de Zimri-Lim," *NABU* 1 (1998): 35–37; see *CAD* A/2, 93–95; *AHw* 46.

8. Besides Amorites from the northwest, Ur also had to contend with the Elamites and the Hurrians and Subarians from east of the Tigris; see Gadd, "Babylonia," 595–643, esp. 624–25.

9. See ch. 2 above; Kupper, *Les Nomades En Mésopotamie,* 149–51; Buccellati, *Amorites of The Ur III Period,* 332–36.

10. Samuel N. Kramer, "The Marriage of Martu," in *Bar-Ilan Studies in Assyriology: Dedicated to Pinhas Artzi* (ed. Jacob Klein and Aaron J. Skaist; Ramat Gan: Bar-Ilan University Press, 1990), 11–27, lines 133–138; and see *PSD* B, 10a. See also a Shu-Sin inscription: "Since that time, the Amorites, a ravaging people, with the instincts of a beast, like wolves, . . . the stalls. A people (who do not know grain)" (Frayne, *Ur III Period,* 299, E3/2.1.4.1, lines v 24–29.

11. Jean-Claude Margueron, "Mari," *OEANE* 3:413–17.

12. The latter are frequently referred to simply as "Benjaminites" because of the similar use of *ben-yəmînî* in the Hebrew Bible.

13. Daniel E. Fleming, "Mari and the Possibilities of Biblical Memory," *RA* 92 (1998): 41–78, esp. 54.

14. Jacob J. Finkelstein, "The Genealogy of the Hammurapi Dynasty," *JCS* 20 (1966): 95–118; Dominique Charpin and Jean-Marie Durand, "Fils de Sim'al: Les origines tribales des rois de Mari," *RA* 80 (1986): 141–86, esp. 159–73.

15. Dominique Charpin, "The History of Ancient Mesopotamia: An Overview," *CANE* 2:807–29, esp. 812–13. While the power of the old "temple economies" persisted, the new cultural conditions witnessed in addition to them a vigorous growth of private enterprise (see below).

16. Sumerian was dead or nearly dead already in the Neo-Sumerian period; see Jerrold S. Cooper, "Sumerian and Akkadian," 239–46, esp. 241. The date of language death is, of course,

difficult to determine with precision, and it is possible that pockets of Sumerian speakers continued in the south into the Old Babylonian period; see Thomsen, *Sumerian Language*, 17–19.

17. For names and dates of the kings in both dynasties, see Charpin, "History of Ancient Mesopotamia," 814–15. For overview, the volume by Edzard is still valuable: Dietz O. Edzard, *Die zweite Zwischenzeit Babyloniens* (Wiesbaden: Harrassowitz, 1957).

18. See Gadd, "Babylonia," 631 and 631–38 for more on what follows.

19. Martha T. Roth, "The Laws of Lipit-Ishtar," *COS* 2.154:410–14; Roth, *Law Collections*, 22–35.

20. Frayne, *Sargonic and Gutian Periods*, 8; Westenholz, *Legends of the Kings of Akkade*.

21. These have been collected and edited by Arthur Ungnad, "Datenlisten," *RlA* 2:131–94, esp. 147–92, and selected ones are translated in A. L. Oppenheim, "Texts from Hammurabi to the Downfall of the Assyrian Empire," *ANET*, 269–301. The use of year-names in Babylonia is distinct from the Assyrian practice of using *limmu* eponym lists for each year, which contain the name and rank of a high official for each year, occasionally including additional references to notable events. On the king lists used here, see A. K. Grayson, "Königslisten und Chroniken, B: Akkadisch," *RlA* 6:86–135, esp. 89–100.

22. Ungnad, "Datenlisten," 175–76.

23. Jack M. Sasson, "King Hammurabi of Babylon," *CANE* 2:901–15, esp. 905.

24. Gadd, "Babylonia," 641–42.

25. Douglas Frayne, *Old Babylonian Period (2003–1595 BC)* (RIME 4; Toronto: University of Toronto Press, 1990), 270 and 280–85, E4.2.14.8–10; Ungnad, "Datenlisten," 162; Gadd, "Babylonia," 642.

26. Astronomical evidence related to the dating of the Old Babylonian period may eventually lead us to accept the so-called high chronology, moving Hammurapi's reign to 1848–1806 B.C.E. and the fall of the dynasty to 1651 instead of 1595; see Peter J. Huber and Abraham Sachs, *Astronomical Dating of Babylon I and Ur III* (Monographic Journals of the Near East 1/4; Malibu, Calif.: Undena Publications, 1982), 3–4 and 42–47; see also my note on chronology in the preface.

27. For summary of this and other issues related to Hammurapi's name, see Sasson, "King Hammurabi of Babylon," esp. 902.

28. Georges Dossin, "Les archives épistolaires du palais de Mari," *Syria* 19 (1938): 105–26, esp. 117–18; J. M. Munn-Rankin, "Diplomacy in Western Asia in the Early Second Millennium B.C.," *Iraq* 18 (1956): 68–110, esp. 108–10.

29. See Oppenheim, "Texts from Hammurabi," 270.

30. Kuhrt, *Ancient Near East*, 1:109.

31. Oppenheim, "Texts from Hammurabi," 269.

32. Dietz O. Edzard, "The Old Babylonian Period," in *The Near East: The Early Civilizations* (ed. Jean Bottéro, Elena Cassin, and Jean Vercoutter; trans. R. F Tannenbaum; The Weidenfeld and Nicolson Universal History 2; London: Weidenfeld & Nicolson, 1967), 177–231, esp. 204.

33. Hartmut Schmökel, *Hammurabi von Babylon: Die Errichtung eines Reiches* (Libelli 330; Darmstadt: Wissenschaftliche Buchgesellschaft, 1975); Horst Klengel, *Hammurapi von Babylon und seine Zeit* (Berlin: Deutscher Verlag der Wissenschaften, 1976); and Franz M. T. Böhl, *Opera Minora Studies en Bijdragen op Assyriologisch en Oudtestamentisch Terrein* (Groningen: Wolters, 1953), 344.

34. Oppenheim, "Texts from Hammurabi," esp. 270.

35. The many letters to Zimri-Lim from his ambassadors at the royal court in Babylon also reveal fascinating features of Hammurapi's temperamental personality and his penchant for micromanagement. For an interesting taste of a number of these letters, see Sasson, "King Hammurabi of Babylon," 908–11; Samuel A. Meier, "Hammurapi," *ABD* 3:39–42, esp. 40–41.

36. Sasson, "King Hammurabi of Babylon," 911.

37. Martha T. Roth, "Laws of Hammurabi," 335–53, esp. 336–37; Roth, *Law Collections,* 76–81; Theophile J. Meek, "The Code of Hammurabi," *ANET,* 163–80, esp. 164–65.

38. Oppenheim, "Texts from Hammurabi," 270.

39. Ibid., 271.

40. Amanda H. Podany, *The Land of Hana: Kings, Chronology, and Scribal Tradition* (Bethesda, Md: CDL Press, 2002), 54–56.

41. For his year-names, see Ungnad, "Datenlisten," esp. 182–85; translated by Oppenheim, "Texts from Hammurabi," 271.

42. For collection of all relevant texts, see F. R. Kraus, *Königliche Verfügungen in altbabylonischer Zeit* (Studia et documenta ad iura Orientis antiqui pertinentia 11; Leiden: Brill, 1984). See also Dominique Charpin, "Les Décrets royaux à l'époque paléo-babylonienne, à propos d'un ouvrage récent," *AfO* 34 (1987): 36–44; for later parallels, see Niels P. Lemche, "Andurârum and Mîšarum: Comments on the Problem of Social Edicts and Their Application in the Ancient Near East," *JNES* 38 (1979): 11–22.

43. Kraus, *Königliche Verfügungen,* esp. 32–35; William W. Hallo, "The Edicts of Samsu-iluna and His Successors," *COS* 2.134:362–64.

44. Hallo, "Edicts of Samsu-iluna and His Successors," 362.

45. The practice of debt release for the impoverished free citizen may have its origins in Amorite tribal or seminomadic culture, which would explain its more frequent use in the Old Babylonian period. Some have further suggested such origins may also explain the presence of this shared feature in Israelite law (Exod 21:2–5 and Deut 15:12–18; compare ¶117 in Hammurapi's Code); see Samuel Greengus, "Biblical and Mesopotamian Law: An Amorite Connection?" in *Life and Culture in the Ancient Near East* (ed. Richard E. Averbeck, Mark W. Chavalas, and David B. Weisberg; Bethesda, Md.: CDL Press, 2003), 63–81, esp. 75–76.

46. Or, 1499 B.C.E., following Gasche, *Dating the Fall of Babylon,* 77–92.

47. Joan Oates, *Babylon* (2nd ed.; New York: Thames & Hudson, 1986), 67.

48. Van De Mieroop estimates each text type (administrative, legal, epistolary, historiographic, literary, and scholastic) at over one hundred, or his "common"; see Van De Mieroop, *Cuneiform Texts,* 11–12.

49. As an agglutinative language (i.e., noninflected, using prefixes or suffixes on a typically monosyllabic verbal root), Sumerian was well suited for pictographic writing, while Semitic languages are morphologically precise, using internal inflections to denote grammatical data. Therefore, Akkadian writers adapted the cuneiform script to use signs more syllabically, and by the Old Babylonian period the syllabic uses of cuneiform signs existed alongside the ideographic and determinative uses; see Cooper, "Sumerian and Akkadian," 239–46; Walker, *Cuneiform,* 15–16; Postgate, *Early Mesopotamia,* 64–65.

50. Benjamin R. Foster, *Before the Muses: An Anthology of Akkadian Literature* (2nd ed.; Potomac, Md.: CDL Press, 1996), 49–59.

51. C. J. Gadd, "Hammurabi and the End of His Dynasty," *CAH*[3] 2/1:176–227, esp. 210–12.

52. Walker, *Cuneiform,* 33–36; for more on the nature of scribal education, see Hartmut Waetzoldt, "Der Schreiber als Lehrer in Mesopotamien," in *Schreiber, Magister, Lehrer: Zur Geschichte und Funktion eines Berufsstandes* (ed. Johann G. Hohenzollern and Max Liedtke; Schriftenreihe zum Bayerischen Schulmuseum Ichenhausen, Zweigmuseum des Bayerischen Nationalmuseums 8; Bad Heilbrunn: Klinkhardt, 1989), 33–50.

53. Åke W. Sjöberg, "The Old Babylonian Edubba," in *Sumerological Studies in Honor of Thorkild Jacobsen on His Seventieth Birthday, June 7, 1974* (ed. Stephen J. Lieberman; AS 20; Chicago: University of Chicago Press, 1976), 159–79; Miguel Civil, "Education in Mesopotamia," *ABD* 2:301–5; and Karen R. Nemet-Nejat, *Daily Life in Ancient Mesopotamia* (Westport, Conn.: Greenwood, 1998), 54–62.

54. Postgate, *Early Mesopotamia,* 69.

55. But see the reservations about using such a distinction in Gadd, "Hammurabi and the End," 213.

56. Tigay, *Evolution of the Gilgamesh Epic,* 241–50; Stephanie Dalley, *Myths from Mesopotamia: Creation, the Flood, Gilgamesh, and Others* (2nd ed.; Oxford: Oxford University Press, 2000), 45–46.

57. However, the Old Babylonian version has only an abbreviated prologue, lacked, of course, the twelfth tablet, which was a very late addition, and may have lacked also the flood story of tablet eleven; see William L. Moran, "The Gilgamesh Epic: A Masterpiece from Ancient Mesopotamia," *CANE* 4:2327–36, esp. 2328–30; Dalley, *Myths from Mesopotamia,* 45.

58. The Epic is available now in a number of English translations: Andrew George, *The Epic of Gilgamesh: The Babylonian Epic Poem and Other Texts in Akkadian and Sumerian* (London: Penguin, 2003); Maureen G. Kovacs, *The Epic of Gilgamesh* (Stanford, Calif.: Stanford University Press, 1989); David Ferry, *Gilgamesh: A New Rendering in English Verse* (New York: Farrar, Straus & Giroux, 1992); Dalley, *Myths from Mesopotamia,* 39–153; Danny P. Jackson, *The Epic of Gilgamesh* (Wauconda, Ill.: Bolchazy-Carducci Publishers, 1992); Benjamin R. Foster, Douglas Frayne, and Gary M. Beckman, *The Epic of Gilgamesh: A New Translation, Analogues, Criticism* (New York: Norton, 2001); E. A. Speiser, "Akkadian Myths and Epics," *ANET,* 60–119, esp. 72–99; A. K. Grayson, "Akkadian Myths and Epics," *ANET,* 503–7; for only the last of the tenth and all of the eleventh tablet, see J. V. Kinnier Wilson, "The Story of the Flood," in *Documents from Old Testament Times* (ed. D. W. Thomas; New York: Harper & Row, 1961), 17–26; Foster, "Epic of Creation," 390–402; for a critical edition of the Standard Version, see Simo Parpola, *The Standard Babylonian Epic of Gilgamesh: Cuneiform Text, Transliteration, Glossary, Indices and Sign List* (SAA Cuneiform Texts 1; Helsinki: Neo-Assyrian Text Corpus Project, 1997). See also Karl Hecker, "Das akkadische Gilgamesch-Epos," *TUAT* 3/4:646–744.

59. According to the Old Babylonian version, tablet X, column iii; see Dalley, *Myths from Mesopotamia,* 150. This is a passage often compared to Eccl 9:7–9.

60. The Standard Babylonian version is from approximately 1100 B.C.E.; see Thorkild Jacobsen, *The Treasures of Darkness: A History of Mesopotamian Religion* (New Haven: Yale University Press, 1976), 208–15; Tigay, *Evolution of the Gilgamesh Epic;* Kramer, *History Begins at Sumer,* 148–53; and David Damrosch, *The Narrative Covenant Transformations of Genre in the Growth of Biblical Literature* (Ithaca, N.Y.: Cornell University Press, 1991), 88–143.

61. Jean Bottéro, *Mesopotamia: Writing, Reasoning, and the Gods* (trans. Zainab Bahrani and Marc Van De Mieroop; Chicago: University of Chicago Press, 1992), 22.

62. This makes any attempt on the part of today's readers to identify specific floods in antiquity as the source of Utnapishtim's account a most hazardous enterprise.

63. Dalley, *Myths from Mesopotamia,* 4–8.

64. Although it may have been composed in the Old Babylonian period and may be of Semitic derivation rather than authentically Sumerian. See Miguel Civil, "The Sumerian Flood Story," in W. G. Lambert, A. R. Millard, and Miguel Civil, *Atra-hasis: The Babylonian Story of the Flood* (Winona Lake, Ind.: Eisenbrauns, 1999), 138–45; Samuel N. Kramer, "The Deluge," *ANET,* 42–44; Thorkild Jacobsen, "The Eridu Genesis," *COS* 1.158:513–15; Jacobsen, *The Harps That Once—: Sumerian Poetry in Translation* (New Haven: Yale University Press, 1987), 145–50.

65. Thorkild Jacobsen, "The Eridu Genesis," *JBL* 100 (1981): 513–29.

66. Lambert, Millard, and Civil, *Atra-hasis;* Dalley, *Myths from Mesopotamia,* 1–38; Benjamin R. Foster, "Atra-hasis," *COS* 1.130:450–53; Wolfram von Soden, "Der altbabylonische Atramchasis-Mythos," *TUAT* 3/4:612–45.

67. Roth, *Law Collections,* 71–142; Meek, "Code of Hammurabi," 163–80; André Finet, *Le code de Hammurapi* (LAPO; Paris: Cerf, 1973); Hans J. Boecker, *Law and the Administration*

of Justice in the Old Testament and Ancient East (Minneapolis: Augsburg, 1980), 67–133; Godfrey R. Driver and John C. Miles, *The Babylonian Laws* (2 vols.; Oxford: Clarendon, 1952–55), 2:1–304; M. E. J. Richardson, *Hammurabi's Laws: Text, Translation and Glossary* (Biblical Seminar, Semitic Texts and Studies 73/2; Sheffield: Sheffield Academic Press, 2000), 28–135; Riekle Borger, "Der Codex Hammurapi," *TUAT* 1/1:39–80.

68. Postgate, *Early Mesopotamia,* 289.

69. For more, and a survey of the role of women in the code, see Kuhrt, *Ancient Near East,* 1:113–15. For more general survey, see Zainab Bahrani, *Women of Babylon: Gender and Representation in Mesopotamia* (London: Routledge, 2001).

70. Postgate, *Early Mesopotamia,* 275–87 and 291. For discussion of one such possible reference to the Code, see Kuhrt, *Ancient Near East,* 1:112.

71. Raymond Westbrook, "Cuneiform Law Codes and the Origins of Legislation," *ZA* 79 (1989): 200–222; Jacob J. Finkelstein, "Some New *misharum* Material and Its Implications," in *Studies in Honor of Benno Landsberger on His Seventy-Fifth Birthday, April 21, 1965* (Chicago: University of Chicago Press, 1965), 223–46.

72. Herbert Petschow, "Die ¶¶ 45 und 46 des Codex Hammurapi," *ZA* 74 (1984): 181–212.

73. Lines xlvii.59–78; Roth, *Law Collections,* 133–34; Roth, "Laws of Hammurabi," 351; Meek, "Code of Hammurabi," 178.

74. Stephen A. Kaufman, "The Second Table of the Decalogue and the Implicit Categories of Ancient Near Eastern Law," in *Love and Death in the Ancient Near East: Essays in Honor of Marvin H. Pope* (ed. John H. Marks and Robert M. Good; Guilford, Conn: Four Quarters, 1987), 111–16.

75. The secondary literature on these topics is large, and I offer here only a sampling. For the Amorite bridge, see George Mendenhall, "Amorites," *ABD* 1:199–202, esp. 202; Abraham Malamat, "The Cultural Impact of the West (Syria-Palestine) on Mesopotamia in the Old Babylonian Period," *AfO* 24 (1997): 310–19.

76. E.g., Thomas L. Thompson, *The Historicity of the Patriarchal Narratives: The Quest for the Historical Abraham* (BZAW 133; Berlin: de Gruyter, 1974), 315–26; Israel Finkelstein and Neil A. Silberman, *The Bible Unearthed: Archaeology's New Vision of Ancient Israel and the Origin of Its Sacred Texts* (New York: Free Press, 2001), 319–21.

77. Greengus, "Biblical and Mesopotamian Law," 67–79.

78. Although much debated, it seems likely that the differences between the Neo-Sumerian monetary penalties for injuries and the Code's use of talionic physical punishments may find origins in the "traditional law of the desert" of Amorite culture; see Postgate, *Early Mesopotamia,* 290.

79. Nemet-Nejat, *Daily Life in Ancient Mesopotamia,* 196–204.

80. Robert D. Biggs, "The Babylonian Prophecies and the Astrological Traditions of Mesopotamia," *JCS* 37 (1985): 86–90; Hermann Hunger and Stephen A. Kaufman, "A New Akkadian Prophecy Text," *JAOS* 95 (1975): 371–75.

81. Maria deJong Ellis, "Observations on Mesopotamian Oracles and Prophetic Texts: Literary and Historiographic Considerations," *JCS* 41 (1989): 127–86; Abraham Malamat, *Mari and the Early Israelite Experience* (The Schweich Lectures of the British Academy 1984; Oxford: Published for the British Academy by the Oxford University Press, 1989), 70–121.

82. For more definition and recent bibliography, see Martti Nissinen, *Prophets and Prophecy in the Ancient Near East* (SBLWAW 12; Atlanta: Society of Biblical Literature, 2003), 1–11. We now have the first known cognate to the Hebrew word for "prophet" (*nābî'*) in texts from Emar and Mari; see Daniel E. Fleming, "The Etymological Origins of the Hebrew *Nābî'*: The One Who Invokes God," *CBQ* 55 (1993): 217–24; Fleming, "*Nābû* and *Munabbiātu:* Two New Syrian Religious Personnel," *JAOS* 113 (1993): 175–83. For a different view, see John Huehnergard, "On the Etymology and Meaning of Hebrew *Nābî'*," *ErIsr* 26 (1999): 88–93.

83. Nissinen, *Prophets and Prophecy,* 94; J. J. M. Roberts, "The Mari Prophetic Texts in Transliteration and English Translation," in *The Bible and the Ancient Near East: Collected Essays* (Winona Lake, Ind: Eisenbrauns, 2002), 157–253, esp. 250–51.

84. H. W. F. Saggs, *The Greatness That Was Babylon: A Survey of the Ancient Civilization of the Tigris-Euphrates Valley* (2nd ed.; London: Sidgwick & Jackson, 1988), 449; Gadd, "Hammurabi and the End," 217–18.

85. For introduction to the topic, see Saggs, *Greatness That Was Babylon,* 420–27.

86. Erica Reiner and David E. Pingree, *Enuma Anu Enlil: The Venus Tablet of Ammisaduqa* (BMes 2/1; Malibu, Calif: Undena Publications, 1975).

87. Gasche, *Dating the Fall of Babylon;* Frederick H. Cryer, "Chronology: Issues and Problems," *CANE* 2:651–64, esp. 658–69.

88. Jacobsen, *Treasures of Darkness.* Among his several other important publications on this topic, see Jacobsen, "Mesopotamia," in *Before Philosophy: The Intellectual Adventure of Ancient Man, An Essay on Speculative Thought in the Ancient Near East* (ed. Henri Frankfort and H. A. Groenewegen-Frankfort; Harmondsworth, U.K.: Penguin, 1964), 137–234.

89. Oppenheim, *Ancient Mesopotamia,* 171–83, a position taken partly as a reaction to the early writings of Jacobsen.

90. In his attempt to demonstrate that the cultural continuum between us and ancient Mesopotamian religion is not as absolute as Oppenheim supposed, Saggs overemphasized the continuum between ancient Israel and Babylonia; see H. W. F. Saggs, *The Encounter with the Divine in Mesopotamia and Israel* (Jordan Lectures in Comparative Religion 12; London: Athlone, 1978), 1–29.

91. Jeremy A. Black and Anthony R. Green, *Gods, Demons, and Symbols of Ancient Mesopotamia: An Illustrated Dictionary* (Austin: University of Texas Press, 1992), 93–98 and 147; Helmer Ringgren, *Religions of the Ancient Near East* (trans. John Sturdy; Philadelphia: Westminster, 1973), 52–68; on earlier Semitic religion, see J. J. M. Roberts, *The Earliest Semitic Pantheon: A Study of the Semitic Deities Attested in Mesopotamia before Ur III* (Baltimore: Johns Hopkins University Press, 1972), 152–54.

92. Wilfred G. Lambert, "Ancient Mesopotamian Gods: Superstition, Philosophy, Theology," *RHR* 207 (1990): 115–30, esp. 119–20 for this reconstruction and for what follows.

93. Postgate, *Early Mesopotamia,* 265–66; Saggs, *Greatness That Was Babylon,* 329–38.

94. Elizabeth C. Stone, "Ziggurat," 390–91, esp. 390.

95. C. B. F. Walker and Michael B. Dick, *The Induction of the Cult Image in Ancient Mesopotamia: The Mesopotamian Mis Pî Ritual* (SAA Literary Texts 1; Helsinki: University of Helsinki, 2001), 6–7; Oppenheim, *Ancient Mesopotamia,* 186; Saggs, *Greatness That Was Babylon,* 309. See also Isa 44:12–20 and Hab 2:18–20.

CHAPTER 4

1. John A. Brinkman, "Meerland," *RlA* 8:6–10, esp. 6–8.

2. Following again the so-called "middle chronology," as stated in the preface. For a recent alternative, see Gasche, *Dating the Fall of Babylon.* In addition to Hittite sources, the sack of Babylon is recorded in a later Babylonian chronicle, which is an important chronological connection; see Glassner, *Mesopotamian Chronicles,* 273; Grayson, *Assyrian and Babylonian Chronicles,* 156, Chronicle 20B, rev. 11–14; for discussion, see O. R. Gurney, "Anatolia, c. 1750–1600 B.C.," *CAH³* 2/1:228–55, esp. 249–50.

3. As explained recently by Gwendolyn Leick, *The Babylonians: An Introduction* (London: Routledge, 2002), 42–43.

4. Gasche, *Dating the Fall of Babylon.*

5. Thus, Postgate is justified in writing a socioeconomic history of "Early Mesopotamia," with 1500 B.C.E. as the *terminus ad quem;* see Postgate, *Early Mesopotamia,* xxi–xxii.

6. Brinkman, "Meerland," esp. 6–8.

7. The lifestyle of today's Madan, or Marsh Arabs, is remarkably similar to ancient inhabitants, including their canoes, reed boats, and reed-enforced architecture (Roaf, *Cultural Atlas of Mesopotamia*, 40–42 and 51). However, the introduction of water buffalo may have been much later than Roaf assumes; see Postgate, *Early Mesopotamia*, 6–7.

8. According to a number of Samsu-iluna's year-date formulas; see A. L. Oppenheim, "Texts from Hammurabi," *ANET*, 269–301, esp. 271; C. J. Gadd, "Hammurabi and the End," *CAH*[3] 2/1:176–227, esp. 220–22.

9. Grayson, "Königslisten und Chroniken," 86–135, esp. 90–96; Oppenheim, "Texts from Hammurabi," esp. 272.

10. Walter Sommerfeld, "The Kassites of Ancient Mesopotamia: Origins, Politics, and Culture," *CANE* 2:917–30, esp. 917; Brinkman, "Karduniaš," 423.

11. John A. Brinkman, "Hurrians in Babylonia in the Late Second Millennium B.C.: An Unexploited Minority Resource for Socio-economic and Philological Analysis," in *Studies on the Civilization and Culture of Nuzi and the Hurrians: In Honor of Ernest R. Lacheman* (ed. Martha A. Morrison and David I. Owen; Winona Lake, Ind.: Eisenbrauns, 1981), 27–35, esp. 28.

12. Brinkman, "Karduniaš," esp. 466; Piotr Bienkowski, "Kassites," in *Dictionary of the Ancient Near East* (ed. Piotr Bienkowski and Alan R. Millard; Philadelphia: University of Pennsylvania Press, 2000), 164–65.

13. Kemal Balkan, *Kassitenstudien* (AOS 37; New Haven: American Oriental Society, 1954), esp. 202–34; Brinkman, "Karduniaš," 472–73.

14. The 576 years and 36 kings recorded for the Kassite Dynasty in the Babylonian King List A must include—if close to accurate—rulers long before they controlled Babylon proper; see Grayson, "Königslisten und Chroniken," esp. 92; Oppenheim, "Texts from Hammurabi," 272. They were, in fact, also able to establish a brief kingdom at Hana toward the close of the Old Babylonian period, located at Terqa. Nevertheless, Kassites ruled from Babylon, at least as a ceremonial and religious center, from approximately 1530 B.C.E. until 1155 B.C.E.

15. Although great strides have been taken in that direction by Brinkman in his excellent review of the sources available: John A. Brinkman, *A Catalogue of Cuneiform Sources Pertaining to Specific Monarchs of the Kassite Dynasty* (Materials and Studies for Kassite History 1; Chicago: Oriental Institute of the University of Chicago, 1976); see also Brinkman, "The Monarchy in the Time of the Kassite Dynasty," in *Le Palais et la Royauté: Archéologie et Civilisation* (ed. Paul Garelli; Paris: Geuthner, 1974), 395–408. Most other surveys of Kassite history are chapters contained in larger general works, the best of which is Brinkman, "Karduniaš," 464–73; Kuhrt, *Ancient Near East*, 1:332–48; Sommerfeld, "Kassites of Ancient Mesopotamia"; and Leick, *Babylonians*, 43–54.

16. Brinkman, "Karduniaš," 466.

17. M. B. Rowton, "Chronology, II. Ancient Western Asia," *CAH*[3] 1/1:193–239, esp. 197; Brinkman, *Catalogue of Cuneiform Sources*, 397–414.

18. Note the numerous question marks, omitted names, and uncertain dates in the standard list (Brinkman, *Catalogue of Cuneiform Sources*; Kuhrt, *Ancient Near East*, 1:336).

19. Modern 'Aqar Quf; see Hartmut Kühne, "'Aqar Quf," *OEANE* 1:156–57.

20. Roaf, *Cultural Atlas of Mesopotamia*, 141.

21. Chronicle P 4:3–7; Grayson, *Assyrian and Babylonian Chronicles*, 175–76 (no. 22); Glassner, *Mesopotamian Chronicles*, 281; see J. M. Munn-Rankin, "Assyrian Military Power 1300–1200 B.C.," *CAH*[3] 2/2:274–306, esp. 284–94. The Assyrian perspective is graphically preserved in the Tukulti-Ninurta Epic; see A. K. Grayson, Grant Frame, Douglas Frayne, and M. P. Maidman, *Assyrian Rulers of the Third and Second Millennia BC (to 1115 BC)* (RIM 1; Toronto: University of Toronto Press, 1987), 231–99; Foster, *Before the Muses*, 209–30.

22. Richard L. Zettler, "12th Century B.C. Babylonia: Continuity and Change," in *The Crisis Years: The 12th Century B.C. From Beyond the Danube to the Tigris* (ed. William A. Ward and Martha S. Joukowsky; Dubuque, Iowa: Kendall/Hunt, 1992), 174–81.

23. Chronicle P records the devastation of most of the cities of Babylonia (Grayson, *Assyrian and Babylonian Chronicles,* 176–77; Glassner, *Mesopotamian Chronicles,* 278–81).

24. Several Elamite records relate details of the campaign, see René Labat, "Elam and Western Persia, c. 1200–1000 B.C.," *CAH³* 2/2:482–506, esp. 485–87.

25. Brinkman, "Karduniaš," 466–69; Brinkman, "Monarchy," 395–408.

26. However, the relative dearth of available texts and the lack of scholarly attention devoted to the Kassite period are caveats often repeated and make this reconstruction tentative; see Sommerfeld, "Kassites of Ancient Mesopotamia," esp. 919–20.

27. Kuhrt, *Ancient Near East,* 1:342–43; Brinkman, "Karduniaš," esp. 467–68.

28. Leick, *Babylonians,* 49–50.

29. Most were composed elsewhere and received by the Egyptian chancery, while eleven letters were composed in Egypt and never sent or filed as copies.

30. Carlo Zaccagnini, "The Interdependence of the Great Powers," in *Amarna Diplomacy: The Beginnings of International Relations* (ed. Raymond Cohen and Raymond Westbrook; Baltimore: Johns Hopkins University Press, 2000), 141–53; William L. Moran, *The Amarna Letters* (Baltimore: Johns Hopkins University Press, 1992), xxii–xxvi.

31. Moran, *Amarna Letters,* EA 2 and EA 3, 6–8.

32. EA 11 and EA 7, respectively (Moran, *Amarna Letters,* 12–16 and 21–23). The marriage of his daughter appears to have gone on as planned.

33. Moran, *Amarna Letters,* EA 9, 18–19.

34. We are unable "to assess specifically Kassite influence on contemporary Babylonia other than at the very top of the political sphere" (Brinkman, "Karduniaš," 467; see also Kuhrt, *Ancient Near East,* 1:338–39).

35. Even cuneiform tablets from this period are similar in script and shape to the Old Babylonian period; see C. B. F. Walker, *Cuneiform,* 17.

36. Brinkman, "Karduniaš," 472.

37. Wilfred G. Lambert, "Ancestors, Authors and Canonicity," *JCS* 11 (1957): 1–14, 112.

38. Leick, *Babylonians,* 49–50; Sommerfeld, "Kassites of Ancient Mesopotamia," 926.

39. Moran, "Gilgamesh Epic," *CANE* 4:2327–36, esp. 2330.

40. Dalley, *Myths from Mesopotamia,* 45.

41. W. G. Lambert, *Babylonian Wisdom Literature* (Winona Lake, Ind.: Eisenbrauns, 1996), 21–62; Wolfram von Soden, "Der leidende Gerechte," *TUAT* 3/1:110–35, esp. 114; Robert D. Biggs, "Akkadian Didactic and Wisdom Literature," *ANET,* 592–607, esp. 596–600; Foster, *Before the Muses,* 306–23; see also Benjamin R. Foster, "The Poem of the Righteous Sufferer," *COS* 1.153:486–92.

42. A second Babylonian theodicy, an elaborate acrostic poem, was probably composed around 1000 B.C.E. and outlines the evils of social injustice while a "friend" attempts to reconcile this with the established views on the divinely ordered justice of the universe. The two finally agree that humans are unjust, and this is because the gods made them so; see Lambert, *Babylonian Wisdom Literature,* 63–90; Biggs, "Akkadian Didactic and Wisdom Literature," esp. 601–4; see also 438–40; Foster, *Before the Muses,* 790–98; and Benjamin R. Foster, *From Distant Days: Myths, Tales, and Poetry of Ancient Mesopotamia* (Bethesda, Md.: CDL Press, 1995), 316–23; Wolfram von Soden, "Die babylonische Theodizee," *TUAT* 3/1:143–57.

43. Sommerfeld, "Kassites of Ancient Mesopotamia," 927–28.

44. Brinkman, "Karduniaš," esp. 471–72.

45. Georges Roux, *Ancient Iraq* (3rd ed.; London: Penguin, 1992), 229–30.

46. The verb *kadāru* III, "to establish a border (by means of a boundary stone)"; see *CAD* K 30–31; *AHw* 419.

47. Ignace J. Gelb, Piotr Steinkeller, and Robert M. Whiting, *Earliest Land Tenure Systems in the Near East: Ancient Kudurrus* (OIP 104; 2 vols.; Chicago: Oriental Institute of the University of Chicago, 1991); John A. Brinkman, "Kudurru; A, Philologisch," *RlA* 6:267–74; Ursula Seidl, "Kudurru; B, Bildschmuck," *RlA* 6:275–77; Nemet-Nejat, *Daily Life in Ancient Mesopotamia,* 261–63.

48. This genre continued until approximately the middle of the first millennium B.C.E., although the contents of the inscriptions evolved significantly (Brinkman, "Kudurru," 274).

49. Sommerfeld, "Kassites of Ancient Mesopotamia," esp. 920–25.

50. C. J. Gadd, "Assyria and Babylon, c. 1370–1300 B.C.," *CAH*³ 2/2:21–48, esp. 44–48.

51. Sommerfeld, "Kassites of Ancient Mesopotamia," esp. 918.

CHAPTER 5

1. So, although "Neo-Babylonian" denotes the later period under review in ch. 6 below, linguistically it refers to the Akkadian dialect in southern Mesopotamia from roughly the end of the second millennium B.C.E. to the mid-sixth century B.C.E. (*CAD* Ḫ vi). The designation "Standard Babylonian" refers to the literary language in which scribes in both Babylonia and Assyria attempted to duplicate Old Babylonian as the classical period of Akkadian literature. This is the dialect used for the *Enūma Eliš* and other important literary compositions of the late second and the first millennia B.C.E., as well as many royal inscriptions. For letters and other nonliterary texts of this period, Woodington prefers "Standard or High Neo-Babylonian" as a dialect within the Neo-Babylonian language generally, which she maintains is distinctive enough to be considered a separate language (Nancy R. Woodington, "A Grammar of the Neo-Babylonian Letters of the Kuyunjik Collection" [Ph.D. diss., Yale University, 1982], 2). Huehnergard uses "Neo-Babylonian" for the dialect in the south to the fall of the Assyrian Empire and "Late Babylonian" for the final periods of written Babylonian texts (Huehnergard, *Grammar of Akkadian,* xxiv–xxv and 595–98).

2. Alternately, "Middle Babylonian period" is used by some to include these centuries down to the beginnings of the Neo-Babylonian Empire, in which case it focuses on the political developments, while missing the significant cultural and linguistic data.

3. Robert Drews, *The End of the Bronze Age: Changes in Warfare and the Catastrophe ca. 1200 B.C.* (Princeton, N.J.: Princeton University Press, 1993), 3.

4. Of course, "nationalism" narrowly defined is an inappropriate designation for ancient Near Eastern ideology. But as we shall see in ch. 6, the concept is useful when discussing sociopolitical developments in Mesopotamia during the first millennium B.C.E.

5. Additional evidence has added others to this list. Vocalization of their names is quite tentative; see Robert Drews, "Medinet Habu: Oxcarts, Ships, and Migration Theories," *JNES* 59 (2000): 161–90, esp. 177–82; and Kuhrt, *Ancient Near East,* 2:387. Maspero articulated his theory in a number of contexts but most prominently in volume 2 of his three-volume *Histoire ancienne des peuples de l'Orient classique* (Paris: Hachette et cie, 1895–99), reprinted as recently as 1968 (Graz: Akademische Druck- und Verlagsanstalt, 1968).

6. Drews, "Medinet Habu," esp. 182–84.

7. For summary of explanations, see Drews, *End of the Bronze Age,* 33–93. Drews himself credits the collapse to revolutionary military innovations—a new style of warfare that opened possibilities for the small groups raiding the Levant (95–225).

8. Distinct in language and less so in culture, ancient Elam, located in today's southwestern Iran, periodically played a significant role in Babylonian history; see I. M. Diakonoff, "Elam," *Cambridge History of Iran* 2:1–24; Kuhrt, *Ancient Near East,* 1:365–74.

9. Zettler, "12th Century B.C. Babylonia," 174–81.

10. H. W. F. Saggs, *The Might That Was Assyria* (London: Sidgwick & Jackson, 1984), 61–62.

11. Robert M. Adams, *The Heartland of Cities: Surveys of Ancient Settlement and Land Use on the Central Floodplain of the Euphrates* (Chicago: University of Chicago Press, 1981), 18, 152, 155–58; for general trends in the demographic base of Babylonian society during the period, see Brinkman, *Prelude to Empire,* 3–10.

12. Kuhrt, *Ancient Near East,* 1:348–55; Gadd, "Assyria and Babylon," 21–48, esp. 23–31.

13. Moran, *Amarna Letters,* 18–19.

14. Grayson, Frame, Frayne, and Maidman, *Assyrian Rulers,* 231 99; Foster, *Before the Muses,* 209–30; see Peter Machinist, "Literature as Politics: The Tukulti-Ninurta Epic and the Bible," *CBQ* 38 (1976): 460–82.

15. John A. Brinkman, *A Political History of Post-Kassite Babylonia, 1158–722 B.C.* (AnOr 43; Rome: Pontifical Biblical Institute, 1968), 260–85; John A. Brinkman, "Babylonia c. 1000–748 B.C.," *CAH²* 3/1:282–313, esp. 288–90.

16. John A. Brinkman, "Foreign Relations of Babylonia from 1600 to 625 B.C.: The Documentary Evidence," *AJA* 76 (1972): 271–81, esp. 278.

17. Alternatively, it is possible that Isin was the first capital of the new ruling house; see John A. Brinkman, "Isin," *RlA* 5:183–89, esp. 184.

18. Grayson, "Königslisten und Chroniken," 86–135, esp. 90–96; Oppenheim, "Texts from Hammurabi," 269–301, esp. 272; see also Brinkman, "Isin," 184.

19. David B. Weisberg, *Texts from the Time of Nebuchadnezzar* (YOS 17; New Haven: Yale University Press, 1980), xix–xxiv; M. P. Streck, "Nebukadnezzar III und IV," *RlA* 9:206.

20. For the meaning of the name, see *AHw* 500; *CAD* K 497; and M. P. Streck, "Nebukadnezar II; A, Historisch," *RlA* 9:194–201, esp. 196.

21. Roth, *Law Collections,* 76; Meek, "Code of Hammurabi," 163–80, esp. 164.

22. This event loomed so large in the minds of ancient Babylonians that it left a veritable library of documentation, including contemporary historical inscriptions of Nebuchadnezzar, epic literature, hymnic and omen literature, and one prophecy. For survey of the literature, see J. J. M. Roberts, "Nebuchadnezzar I's Elamite Crisis in Theological Perspective," in *Essays on the Ancient Near East in Memory of Jacob Joel Finkelstein* (ed. Maria deJong Ellis; Memoirs of the Connecticut Academy of Arts and Sciences 19; Hamden, Conn.: Published for the Academy by Archon Books, 1977), 183–87; repr. in Roberts, *Bible and the Ancient Near East,* 83–92. On the religious significance of the return of Marduk's statue, see Wilfred G. Lambert, "The Reign of Nebuchadnezzar I: A Turning Point in the History of Ancient Mesopotamian Religion," in *The Seed of Wisdom: Essays in Honour of T. J. Meek* (ed. William S. McCullough; Toronto: University of Toronto Press, 1964), 3–13; Walter Sommerfeld, *Der Aufstieg Marduks: Die Stellung Marduks in der babylonischen Religion des zweiten Jahrtausends v. Chr* (AOAT 213; Kevelaer: Butzon & Bercker, 1982). On the important role of the *Enūma Eliš* in this process, see below.

23. Brinkman, "Isin," 186.

24. Ibid., 186–87.

25. Babylonian King List A records several names for rulers of these dynasties in fragmentary fashion; see Oppenheim, "Texts from Hammurabi," esp. 272; Grayson, "Königslisten und Chroniken," esp. 90–96. For a convenient list of rulers, see Kuhrt, *Ancient Near East,* 1:376. On the Bazi and Elamite Dynasties, see Brinkman, "Babylonia," esp. 296–98.

26. Oppenheim, "Texts from Hammurabi," esp. 272; Grayson, "Königslisten und Chroniken," esp. 90–96.

27. Brinkman prefers to speak in general of "uncertain dynasties"; see Brinkman, *Political History of Post-Kassite Babylonia,* 166–213. For details of a few important kings of northwestern Babylonia during the early ninth century, especially Nabu-apla-iddina, see Brinkman, "Babylonia," esp. 301–9.

28. For this assessment, see Brinkman, "Babylonia," esp. 295–309.

29. Chronicle 24, line rev. 8; Grayson, *Assyrian and Babylonian Chronicles,* 182; Glassner, *Mesopotamian Chronicles,* 287. The exact number of years is broken in the text, but Brinkman

argues it is probably at least twelve; see Brinkman, *Political History of Post-Kassite Babylonia,* 213 n. 1327.

30. John A. Brinkman, "Nebukadnezar I," *RlA* 9:192–94, esp. 194.

31. As for example, the Aramaic epigraphs engraved or painted on seventh-century Neo-Assyrian tablets; see Frederick M. Fales, *Aramaic Epigraphs on Clay Tablets of the Neo-Assyrian Period* (Studi semitici: Materiali per il lessico aramaico 2.1; Rome: Università degli studi "La sapienza", 1986); see also John Huehnergard, "What Is Aramaic?" *Aram* 7 (1995): 261–82.

32. Oppenheim, *Ancient Mesopotamia,* 249; Hallo, "Concept of Canonicity," 1–19; the standardization of Babylonian literature into a sort of literary "canon" probably occurred around 1200 B.C.E.; see von Soden, "Problem der zeitlichen Einordnung," 14–26.

33. Reiner, "First-Millennium Babylonian Literature," 293–321, esp. 293–95; Paul-Alain Beaulieu, "King Nabonidus and the Neo-Babylonian Empire," *CANE* 2:969–79, esp. 969–70.

34. Alan R. Millard, "Nabû," *DDD²,* 607–10, esp. 607–8.

35. Being the first words of the composition: "When on high..."; Dalley, *Myths from Mesopotamia,* 228–77; Foster, *Before the Muses,* 351–402; Foster, "Epic of Creation," 390–402; Wilfred G. Lambert, "Enuma Elisch," *TUAT* 3/4:565–602; Speiser, "Akkadian Myths and Epics," 60–119. The *Enūma Eliš* is not the only creation myth from Babylonia, but it is the longest. An older Babylonian poem, the Epic of Atraḫasis, presents in historical sequence both the creation of humanity and its near extinction in the flood and therefore provokes natural comparisons with Genesis; see Lambert, Millard, and Civil, *Atra-ḫasis;* Dalley, *Myths from Mesopotamia,* 1–38; von Soden, "Der altbabylonische Atramchasis-Mythos," 612–45.

36. Presumably the original, second-millennium version of the account had Enlil as the champion-hero. But with the rise of Marduk at the time of Nebuchadnezzar I, the epic was updated and adapted for this era, as it would be later by the Assyrians, who made Ashur the champion-hero.

37. It is, at present, impossible to date the *Enūma Eliš* on the basis of dialectical particulars since features of the hymnic-epic dialect are not yet found in nonliterary, datable inscriptions; see Dalley, *Myths from Mesopotamia,* 228; on the problems related to dating Babylonian literary compositions generally, see Reiner, "First-Millennium Babylonian Literature," esp. 294–95.

38. Saggs, *Encounter with the Divine,* 58; Lambert, "Reign of Nebuchadnezzar I," 3–13. Some have compared this to the exaltation of Yhwh in the exodus and construction of the tabernacle; see William W. Hallo's editorial comments at *COS* 1.111:391; Victor Hurowitz, *I Have Built You an Exalted House: Temple Building in the Bible in the Light of Mesopotamian and North-West Semitic Writings* (JSOTSup 115; Sheffield: JSOT Press, 1992).

39. Tzvi Abusch, "Marduk," *DDD²,* 543–49, esp. 545–46.

40. Roberts, "Nebuchadnezzar I's Elamite Crisis," 183–87.

41. Especially the Epic of Atraḫasis (see n. 35 above). Another plausible suggestion is that the basic story line is Amorite in origin (tablets I–V) and was brought from the west to Babylonia, where it was compiled and extended during the Kassite period by the materials of tablets VI and VII. At this stage the hero of the story was changed from the West Semitic storm god, Adad (or Hadad), to Marduk. See Dalley, *Myths from Mesopotamia,* 230. Others would argue for a much later date, sometime during the early first millennium B.C.E.; see Abusch, "Marduk," esp. 547.

42. The *akītu* festival is absent in western Semitic cultures, such as Ugarit and the Bible; see Dennis Pardee, *Ritual and Cult at Ugarit* (SBLWAW 10; Atlanta: Society of Biblical Literature, 2002), 234.

43. In a convergence of power and authority in the sole personhood of Marduk, his city Babylon, and the king of Babylon; Jeremy A. Black, "The New Year Ceremonies in Ancient Babylon: 'Taking The Hand of Bel' and a Cultic Picnic," *Religion* 11 (1981): 39–59; Amélie Kuhrt, "Usurpation, Conquest and Ceremonial: From Babylon to Persia," in *Rituals of Royalty:*

Power and Ceremonial in Traditional Societies (ed. David Cannadine and S. R. F. Price; Cambridge: Cambridge University Press, 1987), 20–55.

44. Especially in the so-called Nabonidus Chronicle (chronicle 7, lines ii,6,11,20,24, iii.8); Bill T. Arnold, "The Babylonian Chronicle Series," in Chavalas, *Ancient Near East;* Grayson, *Assyrian and Babylonian Chronicles,* 104–11; Glassner, *Mesopotamian Chronicles,* 235–39.

45. Jonathan Goldstein, *Peoples of an Almighty God: Competing Religions in the Ancient World* (ABRL; New York: Doubleday, 2002), 27–31. Goldstein has proposed that the Babylonians and Israelites were truly "peoples of an almighty god" and that the Egyptians and Zoroastrian Iranians were peoples of a nearly almighty god. One might compare Saggs, *Encounter with the Divine;* and Bottéro, *Mesopotamia,* 211–15.

46. Karel van der Toorn, "Theology, Priests, and Worship in Canaan and Ancient Israel," *CANE* 3:2043–58, esp. 2056–57.

47. Brinkman, "Babylonia," esp. 291–92.

48. Ursula Seidl, *Die Babylonischen Kudurru-Reliefs: Symbole Mesopotamischer Gottheiten* (OBO 87; Fribourg: Universitätsverlag; Göttingen: Vandenhoeck & Ruprecht, 1989), 84–85.

49. P. R. S. Moorey, "Babylonia," in *The Cambridge Ancient History, Plates to Volume III* (Cambridge: Cambridge University Press, 1984), 27–36, esp. 27.

Chapter 6

1. Manfried Dietrich, *Die Aramäer Südbabyloniens in der Sargonidenzeit (700–648)* (AOAT 7; Neukirchen-Vluyn: Neukirchener; Kevelaer: Butzon & Bercker, 1970), 1–6; but see the remarks in John A. Brinkman, "Notes on Arameans and Chaldeans in Southern Babylonia in the Early Seventh Century B.C.," *Or* 46 (1977): 304–25; and Bill T. Arnold, "What Has Nebuchadnezzar to Do with David? On the Neo-Babylonian Period and Early Israel," in Chavalas and Younger, *Mesopotamia and the Bible,* 330–55, esp. 332–36.

2. Brinkman, *Political History of Post-Kassite Babylonia,* 266–67 (esp. n. 1716) and 273–75.

3. Grant Frame, *Babylonia 689–627 B.C.: A Political History* (Uitgaven van het Nederlands Historisch-Archaeologisch Instituut te Istanbul 69; Leiden: Nederlands Historisch-Archaeologisch Instituut te Istanbul, 1992), 33.

4. Brinkman, "Babylonia," 282–313, esp. 288.

5. Saggs, *Might That Was Assyria,* 82–84; A. K. Grayson, "Assyria: Ashur-dan II to Ashurnirari V (934–745 B.C.)," *CAH²* 3/1:238–81, esp. 276–79.

6. Brinkman, *Political History of Post-Kassite Babylonia,* 221–24; Brinkman, "Babylonia," esp. 309–12.

7. Grayson, *Assyrian and Babylonian Chronicles,* 10–24 and 69–111; Bill T. Arnold, "Babylonian Chronicle Series"; for details of Nabonassar's reign, see Brinkman, *Political History of Post-Kassite Babylonia,* 226–34; Brinkman, *Prelude to Empire,* esp. 39–40.

8. Francesca Rochberg-Halton, "New Evidence for the History of Astrology," *JNES* 43 (1984): 115–40, esp. 115.

9. John A. Brinkman and D. A. Kennedy, "Documentary Evidence for the Economic Base of Early Neo-Babylonian Society: A Survey of Dated Babylonian Economic Texts," *JCS* 35 (1983): 1–90; but see the cautions about this evidence in Brinkman, *Prelude to Empire,* 40 n. 199.

10. Brinkman, *Political History of Post-Kassite Babylonia,* 235–40.

11. Saggs, *Might That Was Assyria,* 89–92. Tukulti-Ninurta I (1244–1208) of Assyria had claimed the title "king of Babylon(ia)," but in point of fact he was not recognized as king in the native Babylonian tradition; see John A. Brinkman "Elamite Military Aid to Merodach-Baladan," *JNES* 24 (1965): 161–66, esp. 161 n. 1.

12. John A. Brinkman, "Merodach-baladan II," in *Studies Presented to A. Leo Oppenheim* (ed. Robert D. Biggs and John A. Brinkman; Chicago: Oriental Institute, 1964), 6–53; R. J. van

der Spek, "The Struggle of King Sargon II of Assyria against the Chaldaean Merodach-Baladan (710–707 B.C.)," *JEOL* 25 (1978): 56–66.

13. Brinkman, "Merodach-baladan II," 38–40.

14. John A. Brinkman, "Sennacherib's Babylonian Problem: An Interpretation," *JCS* 25 (1973): 89–95, esp. 90–94. See also Saggs, *Might That Was Assyria*, 99–103.

15. Brinkman, *Prelude to Empire*, 69–70.

16. Ibid., 70–84.

17. Bustenay Oded, "Judah and the Exile," in *Israelite and Judaean History* (ed. John H. Hayes and J. M. Miller; OTL; Philadelphia: Westminster, 1977), 435–88, esp. 454–56. For this among other possibilities, see H. G. M. Williamson, *1 and 2 Chronicles* (NCB; Grand Rapids: Eerdmans, 1982), 391–93.

18. The rise of Assyria also made strange bedfellows in Syria-Palestine, such as Ahab's peace with Ben-Hadad II (1 Kgs 20:31–34) and Pekah's with Rezin (2 Kgs 16:5–7). Further parallels may be found in the Persian threat that unified Greek clans and set the stage for the golden age of Greece.

19. Brinkman, *Prelude to Empire*, 110–11 n. 551. The only source connecting Nabopolassar with the Sealand is late and of questionable reliability; see Donald J. Wiseman, *Nebuchadrezzar and Babylon* (The Schweich Lectures 1983; Oxford: Published for the British Academy by Oxford University Press, 1985), 5–6. The Greeks greatly revered the "Chaldeans" as priests, diviners, and scholars, for their superiority in all things astronomical and mathematical; see Amélie Kuhrt, "Ancient Mesopotamia in Classical Greek and Hellenistic Thought," *CANE* 1:55–65, esp. 61.

20. The most common form of royal inscription from this period; see Richard S. Ellis, *Foundation Deposits in Ancient Mesopotamia* (Yale Near Eastern Researches 2; New Haven: Yale University Press, 1968), 110–13.

21. Farouk N. H. Al-Rawi, "Nabopolassar's Restoration Work on the Wall Imgur-Enlil at Babylon," *Iraq* 47 (1985): 1–13, esp. 3 and 5, lines i 28–ii 5; Paul-Alain Beaulieu, "Nabopolassar's Restoration of Imgur-Enlil, The Inner Defensive Wall of Babylon," *COS* 2.121:307–8; Stephen H. Langdon, *Die neubabylonischen Königsinschriften* (VAB 4; Leipzig: Hinrichs, 1912), 68.

22. Vanderhooft, *Neo-Babylonian Empire*, 23–33.

23. Michael Roaf, "Media and Mesopotamia: History and Architecture," in *Later Mesopotamia and Iran: Tribes and Empires, 1600–539 BC, Proceedings of a Seminar in Memory of Vladimir G. Lukonin* (ed. John Curtis; London: British Museum Press, 1995), 54–66; T. C. Young Jr., "The Early History of the Medes and the Persians and the Achaemenid Empire to the Death of Cambyses," *CAH²* 4:1–52.

24. Chronicle 3, lines 28–30; Arnold, "Babylonian Chronicle Series"; Grayson, *Assyrian and Babylonian Chronicles*, 93; Donald J. Wiseman, *Chronicles of Chaldaean Kings (626–556 B.C.) in the British Museum* (London: British Museum, 1956), 14, 57–59; Glassner, *Mesopotamian Chronicles*, 221. The new alliance was one of "goodwill and good relations [i.e., peace]" (Akkadian *sulummû, AHw* 1057); see Donald J. Wiseman, "'Is it Peace?'—Covenant and Diplomacy," *VT* 32 (1982): 311–26.

25. Wiseman, *Nebuchadrezzar and Babylon*, 13–15; on the spelling of Nebuchadnezzar's name, see ch. 5 above.

26. Langdon, *Neubabylonischen Königsinschriften*, 62–63, ii 71–iii 3; see similar references in chronicle 5, line obverse 1: Arnold, "Babylonian Chronicle Series"; Grayson, *Assyrian and Babylonian Chronicles*, 99–100; Alan R. Millard, "The Babylonian Chronicle," *COS* 1.137:467–68; Glassner, *Mesopotamian Chronicles*, 227.

27. Chronicle 5, lines obverse 10–11; Arnold, "Babylonian Chronicle Series"; Grayson, *Assyrian and Babylonian Chronicles*, 99–100; Millard, "Babylonian Chronicle," 468; Donald J. Wiseman, "Babylonia 605–539 B.C.," *CAH²* 3/2:229–51, esp. 230–31; Glassner, *Mesopotamian*

Chronicles, 229. That Nebuchadnezzar also despoiled the Jerusalem temple before leaving for home, taking Daniel and others into exile, is dependent on Berossus and Dan 1:1, which are open to alternative interpretations; see John J. Collins, *Daniel: A Commentary on the Book of Daniel* (Hermeneia; Minneapolis: Fortress, 1993), 130–33.

28. Chronicle 5, lines obverse 18–19; Arnold, "Babylonian Chronicle Series"; Grayson, *Assyrian and Babylonian Chronicles,* 100; Glassner, *Mesopotamian Chronicles,* 229

29. F g , A. K. Grayson, "Assyria 668–635 B.C.: The Reign of Ashurbanipal," *CAH*[2] 3/2:142–61, esp. 161.

30. Vanderhooft, *Neo-Babylonian Empire,* 90–99; and David S. Vanderhooft, "Babylonian Strategies of Imperial Control in the West: Royal Practice and Rhetoric," in *Judah and the Judeans in the Neo-Babylonian Period* (ed. Oded Lipschitz and Joseph Blenkinsopp; Winona Lake, Ind.: Eisenbrauns, 2003), 235–62.

31. Ronald H. Sack, "Nebuchadnezzar II and the Old Testament: History versus Ideology," in Lipschitz and Blenkinsopp, *Judah and the Judeans,* 221–33, esp. 226–31. The lack of an administrative title for Gedaliah at Mizpah complicates matters, as it might otherwise have indicated the status of Judah immediately following its capture and destruction by Nebuchadnezzar (2 Kgs 25:22–26); see Mordechai Cogan and Hayim Tadmor, *II Kings: A New Translation with Introduction and Commentary* (AB 11; Garden City, N.Y.: Doubleday, 1988), 327.

32. Chronicle 5, lines reverse 6–7; Arnold, "Babylonian Chronicle Series"; Grayson, *Assyrian and Babylonian Chronicles,* 101; Glassner, *Mesopotamian Chronicles,* 229.

33. To the dismay of Jeremiah and a pro-Babylonian party in Jerusalem (Jer 27:6–11).

34. Chronicle 5, lines reverse 11–12; Arnold, "Babylonian Chronicle Series"; Millard, "Babylonian Chronicle," 468; Grayson, *Assyrian and Babylonian Chronicles,* 102; Glassner, *Mesopotamian Chronicles,* 231.

35. Chronicle 5, reverse line 21; Arnold, "Babylonian Chronicle Series"; Grayson, *Assyrian and Babylonian Chronicles,* 102; Wiseman, *Nebuchadrezzar and Babylon,* 34–36; Glassner, *Mesopotamian Chronicles,* 231.

36. Chronicle 5, lines reverse 23–24; Arnold, "Babylonian Chronicle Series"; Grayson, *Assyrian and Babylonian Chronicles,* 102; Glassner, *Mesopotamian Chronicles,* 231.

37. T. G. H. James, "Egypt: The Twenty-Fifth and Twenty-Sixth Dynasties," *CAH*[2] 3/2:677–747, esp. 718–19; on the Nubian campaign, see 726–30.

38. Hayim Tadmor, "The Chronology of the First Temple Period: A Presentation and Evaluation of the Sources," in J. Alberto Soggin, *An Introduction to the History of Israel and Judah* (2nd ed.; Valley Forge, Pa.: Trinity Press International, 1993), 394–417, esp. 404–5.

39. Lachish Ostracon 4; Johannes Renz and Wolfgang Röllig, *Handbuch der althebräischen Epigraphik* (3 vols.; Darmstadt: Wissenschaftliche Buchgesellschaft, 1995–), 1:422; Dennis Pardee, "Lachish Ostraca," *COS* 3.42:78–81, esp. 80.

40. For a defense of this view of the letter, see Anson Rainey, "Watching Out for the Signal Fires of Lachish," *PEQ* 119 (1987): 149–51.

41. David Noel Freedman, *The Unity of the Hebrew Bible* (Distinguished Senior Faculty Lecture Series; Ann Arbor: University of Michigan Press, 1991), esp. 6–7.

42. Ephraim Stern, *Archaeology of the Land of the Bible: The Assyrian, Babylonian, and Persian Periods, 732–332 BCE* (ABRL; New York: Doubleday, 2001), esp. 301–50. Stern avers further that the Babylonians apparently had no interest in governing the region but merely in preventing its unification for purposes of dominance.

43. Charles E. Carter, *The Emergence of Yehud in the Persian Period: A Social and Demographic Study* (JSOTSup 294; Sheffield: Sheffield Academic Press, 1999), 200–201. Oded Lipschitz believes the population of Jerusalem itself, as well as the Shephelah and Negev, dropped dramatically due to the Babylonian devastation, while the region of Benjamin continued to be inhabited, although at approximately 40 percent of its previous population levels. Only 10 percent of the populace lived in Jerusalem and its environs during the exile; see

Oded Lipschitz, "Demographic Changes in Judah between the Seventh and the Fifth Centuries B.C.E.," in Lipschitz and Blenkinsopp, *Judah and the Judeans,* 323–76.

44. M. Broshi and Israel Finkelstein, "The Population of Palestine in Iron Age II," *BASOR* 287 (1992): 47–60. On the debate over the degree of cultural continuity in Judea after the Babylonian conquest, see Hans M. Barstad, "After the 'Myth of the Empty Land': Major Challenges in the Study of Neo-Babylonian Judah," in Lipschitz and Blenkinsopp, *Judah and the Judeans,* 3–20; for responses, see the essays by Lisbeth S. Fried and Bustenay Oded in the same volume (respectively, pages 21–54 and 55–74).

45. Wiseman, "Babylonia," 236; Wiseman, *Nebuchadrezzar and Babylon,* 39–40.

46. Vanderhooft, *Neo-Babylonian Empire,* 33–48.

47. E.g., Paul-Alain Beaulieu, "A New Inscription of Nebuchadnezzar II Commemorating the Restoration of Emaḫ in Babylon," *Iraq* 59 (1997): 93–96.

48. On Babylonian "nationalism" as it was linked to the capital city, Babylon, and as distinct from the royal ideology of Assyria before it and Persia after it, see Deryck C. T. Sheriffs, "'A Tale of Two Cities': Nationalism in Zion and Babylon," *TynBul* 39 (1988): 19–57, esp. 20–38.

49. Evelyn Klengel-Brandt, "Babylon," *OEANE* 1:251–56, esp. 252–53. Herodotus (1.178) asserts, "in addition to its enormous size it surpasses in splendor any city of the known world."

50. During later Babylonian history, the *Enūma Eliš* was quoted on the fourth day of the New Year festival at Babylon, the so-called *akītū* festival, and played a significant role in the religious and social life of the community; Abusch, "Marduk," 543–49, esp. 548.

51. Abraham Sachs, "Temple Program for the New Year's Festivals at Babylon," *ANET,* 331–34.

52. Wilfred G. Lambert, "Nebuchadnezzar King of Justice," *Iraq* 27 (1965): 1–11.

53. Elizabeth C. Stone, "Ziggurat," 390–91.

54. Vanderhooft, *Neo-Babylonian Empire,* 50–51.

55. Burstein, *Babyloniaca of Berossus,* 27; and quoted by Josephus, *Ant.* 10.11.1 §226.

56. Wiseman, *Nebuchadrezzar and Babylon,* 56–60; Beaulieu, "King Nabonidus," 969–79, esp. 971.

57. Roaf, *Cultural Atlas of Mesopotamia,* 193, although Babylon's walls are not universally counted among the "seven."

58. Andrew George, "Babylon Revisited: Archaeology and Philology in Harness," *Antiquity* 67 (1993): 734–46. The town plan presented by Eckhard Unger over seventy years ago and frequently duplicated in the secondary literature should now be replaced by a new sketch map of the city, in light of the advances in coordinating text and tell (ibid., 738–39).

59. The views of William F. Albright on this topic may still be read with profit, if only as an intellectual curiosity; see William F. Albright, *From the Stone Age to Christianity: Monotheism and the Historical Process* (2nd ed.; Baltimore: John Hopkins University Press, 1957), esp. 120–26. However, his three stages of human intellectual development (protological, empirical logic, and analytical logic) should be read in light of the critique of Peter Machinist, "On Self-Consciousness in Mesopotamia," in *The Origins and Diversity of Axial Age Civilizations* (ed. S. N. Eisenstadt; SUNY Series in Near Eastern Studies; Albany: State University of New York Press, 1986), 183–202, esp. 195–200.

60. Evidence that he died in the first week of October 562 has been reassessed in light of indications he may have died a few months earlier; see Ronald H. Sack, *Amēl-Marduk, 562–560 B.C.: A Study Based on Cuneiform, Old Testament, Greek, Latin and Rabbinical Sources* (AOAT 4; Neukirchen-Vluyn: Neukirchener; Kevelaer: Butzon & Bercker, 1972), 3, 90, 106; Weisberg, *Texts from the Time of Nebuchadnezzar,* xix; for summary, see Wiseman, "Babylonia," esp. 240.

61. Paul R. Berger, *Die neubabylonischen Königsinschriften: Königsinschriften des ausgehenden babylonischen Reiches (626–539 a.Chr.)* (AOAT 4/1; Neukirchen-Vluyn: Neukirchener; Kevelaer: Butzon & Bercker, 1973), 94–95.

62. Sack, "Nebuchadnezzar II and the Old Testament," 223.

63. A. L. Oppenheim, "The Neo-Babylonian Empire and Its Successors," *ANET*, 301–17, esp. 308.

64. Certainly there were those in Judah who considered Jehoiachin the legitimate king and Zedekiah only his regent. This was likely behind the prophecy of Hananiah son of Azzur that Jehoiachin would return to Judah within two years, leading a return of exiles and stolen temple vessels (Jer 28:2–4), and it possibly also explains why the book of Ezekiel uses a dating system based on the year of Jehoiachin's deportation (Ezek 1:2).

65. Wiseman, "Babylonia," esp. 240–41.

66. For a different interpretation of the problems involved in Jer 39:3 and 13, see Vanderhooft, *Neo-Babylonian Empire*, 150–51.

67. Sack, *Amēl-Marduk*, 36–39; Wiseman, "Babylonia," esp. 241–42.

68. According to Berossus; Burstein, *Babyloniaca of Berossus*, 28; quoted by Josephus, *Ag. Ap.* 1.146–147; the account of irregularities involved in Neriglissar's rise to the throne have now been confirmed, albeit through fragmentary sources; see Ronald H. Sack, *Neriglissar—King of Babylon* (AOAT 236; Kevelaer: Butzon & Bercker; Neukirchen-Vluyn: Neukirchener, 1994), 23–33.

69. Langdon, *Neubabylonischen Königsinschriften*, 208–19.

70. Chronicle 6, lines 1–27; Arnold, "Babylonian Chronicle Series"; Grayson, *Assyrian and Babylonian Chronicles*, 20–21, 103–4; Glassner, *Mesopotamian Chronicles*, 233.

71. A. L. Oppenheim, "Babylonian and Assyrian Historical Texts," *ANET*, 556–67, esp. 566; Wiseman, "Babylonia," 243.

72. Paul-Alain Beaulieu, *The Reign of Nabonidus, King of Babylon, 556–539 B.C.* (Yale Near Eastern Researches 10; New Haven: Yale University Press, 1989), 67–68.

73. Tremper Longman III, "The Adad-guppi Autobiography," *COS* 1.147:477–78; Oppenheim, "Babylonian and Assyrian Historical Texts," esp. 560–62. Adad-guppi has often been called a high priestess of Sîn, but this goes beyond the available evidence; see Beaulieu, *Reign of Nabonidus*, 68.

74. Chronicle 7, lines ii 13–15; Arnold, "Babylonian Chronicle Series"; Grayson, *Assyrian and Babylonian Chronicles*, 107; Glassner, *Mesopotamian Chronicles*, 237.

75. Beaulieu, *Reign of Nabonidus*, 90–98.

76. Ibid., 138–43.

77. Warwick Ball and Jeremy A. Black, "Excavations in Iraq, 1985–1986," *Iraq* 49 (1987): under "Sippar"; see also Olof Pedersén, *Archives and Libraries in the Ancient Near East, 1500–300 B.C.* (Bethesda, Md.: CDL Press, 1998), 194–97.

78. Kuhrt, *Ancient Near East*, 2:573–74.

79. He appears to have visited Uruk, Larsa, and Ur (Langdon, *Neubabylonischen Königsinschriften*, 284–85, column ix, lines 50–57).

80. Grant Frame, "Nabonidus, Nabû-šarra-uṣur and the Eanna Temple," *ZA* 81 (1991): 37–86, esp. 54–66.

81. For survey of the conjectures regarding Nabonidus's actions, see Beaulieu, *Reign of Nabonidus*, 178–85, esp. 184–85.

82. For this interpretation, see Kuhrt, *Ancient Near East*, 2:600–603. Unfortunately, a rock-relief of a Mesopotamian king in southern Jordan, which has been convincingly attributed to Nabonidus and which presumably narrated details of his campaign in the region, is too badly damaged to be read; see Stephanie Dalley and Anne Goguel, "The Sela' Sculpture: A Neo-Babylonian Rock Relief in Southern Jordan," *ADAJ* 41 (1997): 169–76, esp. 172–75.

83. Perhaps explaining why Belshazzar is the king of Dan 5 instead of Nabonidus and why Daniel is offered the "third" position in the kingdom.

84. The fall of the city is recorded by Herodotus (1.191) and Xenophon (*Cyropaedia* 7.26–37).

85. 4QPrNab; see Florentino García-Martínez, *Qumran and Apocalyptic: Studies on the Aramaic Texts from Qumran* (STDJ 9; Leiden: Brill, 1992), esp. 119–20; Peter W. Flint, "The Daniel Tradition at Qumran," in *The Book of Daniel: Composition and Reception* (ed. John J. Collins and Peter W. Flint; VTSup 83/2; Leiden: Brill, 2001), 2:329–67, esp. 332–38.

86. Wiseman, *Nebuchadrezzar and Babylon,* 103–7.

87. Flint, "Daniel Tradition at Qumran," esp. 363–64; Esther Eshel, "Possible Sources of the Book of Daniel," in Collins and Flint, *Book of Daniel,* 2:387–94; John Day, "The Daniel of Ugarit and Ezekiel and the Hero of the Book of Daniel," *VT* 30 (1980): 174–84.

88. For this argument, see Sack, "Nebuchadnezzar II and the Old Testament," esp. 224–25.

89. Beaulieu, *Reign of Nabonidus,* esp. 43–65; Peter Machinist and Hayim Tadmor, "Heavenly Wisdom," in *The Tablet and the Scroll: Near Eastern Studies in Honor of William W. Hallo* (ed. Mark E. Cohen, Daniel C. Snell, and David B. Weisberg; Bethesda, Md.: CDL Press, 1993), 146–51.

90. Vanderhooft, *Neo-Babylonian Empire,* 51–57.

91. Kuhrt, *Ancient Near East,* 2:600–603; Amélie Kuhrt, "Nabonidus and the Babylonian Priesthood," in *Pagan Priests: Religion and Power in the Ancient World* (ed. Mary Beard and John A. North; London: Duckworth, 1990), 117–55; Wiseman, "Babylonia," esp. 244–45; Leick, *Babylonians,* 66–67.

92. Vanderhooft, *Neo-Babylonian Empire,* 57–59.

93. For speculation on Nabonidus's motives, see Vanderhooft, *Neo-Babylonian Empire,* 58–59. The iconography of Nabonidus's official monuments reflects an intentional effort to distinguish himself from his predecessors; see Dalley and Goguel, "The Sela' Sculpture," esp. 174.

94. The reverse of the text contains a long historical apodosis, in which all but the final "prediction" is a *vaticinium ex eventu.* On the basis of the historical allusions, the text can be dated to a proposed coregency of Nebuchadnezzar and Amēl-Marduk; see Hunger and Kaufman, "New Akkadian Prophecy Text," 371–75; for a different interpretation, see Jonathan Goldstein, "The Historical Setting of the Uruk Prophecy," *JNES* 47 (1988): 43–46.

95. Paul-Alain Beaulieu, "The Historical Background of the Uruk Prophecy," in Cohen, Snell, and Weisberg, *Tablet and the Scroll,* 41–52, esp. 49.

96. Chronicle 7, lines iii 12–16; Arnold, "Babylonian Chronicle Series"; Grayson, *Assyrian and Babylonian Chronicles,* 108–9; Glassner, *Mesopotamian Chronicles,* 237–39; Mordechai Cogan, "Cyrus Cylinder," *COS* 2.124:314–16, esp. 315; see also Amélie Kuhrt, "Babylonia from Cyrus to Xerxes," *CAH*² 4:112–38, esp. 120–25.

INDEX OF BIBLICAL REFERENCES

INDEX OF MODERN AUTHORITIES

139

INDEX OF SUBJECTS